THE PUNISHMENT OF GAZA

Described by *Le Monde* as a "thorn in Israel's flank," **Gideon Levy** is a prominent, award-winning Israeli journalist. For over twenty years he has covered the Israel-Palestine conflict, in particular the occupation of Gaza and the West Bank, for the Israeli newspaper *Haaretz* in his column "Twilight Zone."

Israel's 2009 invasion of Gaza was an act of aggression that killed over a thousand Palestinians and devastated the infrastructure of an already impoverished enclave. *The Punishment of Gaza* shows how the ground was prepared for the assault and documents its continuing effects.

From 2005—the year of Gaza's "liberation"—through to 2009, Levy tracks the development of Israeli policy, which has abandoned the pretense of diplomacy in favor of raw military power, the ultimate aim of which is to deny Palestinians any chance to form an independent state. Punished by Israel and the Quartet of international powers for the democratic election of Hamas, Gaza has been transformed into the world's largest open-air prison. From Gazan families struggling to cope with the random violence of Israel's blockade and its "targeted" assassinations, to the machinations of legal experts and the continued connivance of the international community, every aspect of this ongoing tragedy is eloquently recorded and forensically analyzed. Levy's powerful journalism shows how the brutality at the heart of Israel's occupation of Palestine has found its most complete expression to date in the collective punishment of Gaza's residents.

THE PUNISHMENT
OF GAZA

Gideon Levy

VERSO
London • New York

First published by Verso 2010
© Gideon Levy
Translation of Introduction © Revital Sella

3 5 7 9 10 8 6 4

Verso
UK: 6 Meard Street, London W1F 0EG
US: 20 Jay Street, Suite 1010, Brooklyn, NY 11201
www.versobooks.com

Verso is the imprint of New Left Books

ISBN-13: 978-1-84467-601-9

British Library Cataloguing in Publication Data
A catalogue record for this book is available from the British Library

Library of Congress Cataloging-in-Publication Data
A catalog record for this book is available from the Library of Congress

Typeset in Bembo by Hewer Text UK Ltd, Edinburgh
Printed in the US by Quad/Graphics Fairfield

Contents

Part IV: 2009

Introduction

It was a theatrical moment if ever there was one. It happened a long time ago, sometime in the 1990s, after many years of going to Gaza—where I worked and which I love. We stood there, the three of us—Palestinian human rights activist Bassem Eid, my brilliant and steady cameraman Miki Kratsman and myself—on the way out of the Erez checkpoint, which controlled entry and exit from the Strip then as it does now. Those were the euphoric Oslo days, and we (How foolish? How credulous?) thought it was all over, that the occupation had ended, that Gaza was free, liberated. We wouldn't be going there anymore, at least not in the capacity of Sisyphus, as we had done for so many years, to cover the Israeli occupation for an Israeli public that does not want to read, see or hear anything about Gaza. In one rare and unforgettable moment we turned, all three as one, and in a gesture straight out of the movies waved Gaza farewell. Goodbye occupied Gaza, farewell! We are never to meet again, at least not in your occupied state. We shan't be coming to you any more to write up your trials and tribulations, the futile bloodshed and destruction, the humiliation, destitution, deprivation and bereavement that have been your lot for years. Gaza is on a new road, we thought, as we made for Tel Aviv, the most distant point from where we were in the universe, where never a thought is given to Gaza, where its fate never stirs a soul.

Our gesture was misconceived. Very soon we did return to Gaza, to the daily tales of life and death. The occupation did not end. On the contrary, it is more cruel, criminal and inhuman today than ever before. Ten years later, in 2005, when Israel disengaged from Gaza, we were much wiser: this time we knew that the occupation had simply changed form. The jailer pulled out of the jail and was now holding its prisoners captive from without. Yes, Gaza was and still is the largest prison on earth, a gruesome experiment performed on living human beings.

Gaza, my beloved. I've always cherished going there, a statement that to most Israelis sounds lunatic. Since that dramatic wave of farewell, I've been back to Gaza dozens of times. On one occasion a reporter from French television's TF1 channel joined us. In a doorway in Rafah (or was it Khan Younis?) where a paralyzed Palestinian mother lost her only child to an Israeli missile, I said to this French colleague, "This is when I'm ashamed to be Israeli. This horrible missile was launched in my name too." The next day he called me: "We won't be able to broadcast your last remark. It is too extreme. Our audience may take offense." I was deeply distressed. That is precisely what I have been trying to elicit all these years: outrage, outrage and offense at what Israel is making a million and a half helpless immiserated people living in the Strip endure. To the best of my meager abilities, I am asking all Israelis to be outraged—or at least to understand what is being perpetrated in their name, so that they may never have the right to claim: We did not know. We didn't know that the Israeli occupation was so devastating, so brutal; we didn't know this horror was going on.

November 2006 was the last time we were in Gaza. We went to the Indira Gandhi Kindergarten, a private establishment run by a teacher named after the Indian Stateswoman. We arrived during the burial of Najawa Khalif, a twenty-year-old kindergarten teacher killed by another Israeli missile. The school bus had been hit when ferrying the children to this beautifully tended nursery school. Khalif was killed in front of twenty of her wards. On the day we came they were drawing pictures of her lying bleeding on the road, the children huddling terrified beside her, with an Israeli tank shelling from a distance and a plane dropping bombs from above. That is the bloody childhood recollection of the Indira Gandhi Kindergarten kids, and it is my last memory of Gaza. I was no longer allowed to go there. In November 2006 Israel shut down all communication with the Gaza Strip. Israeli journalists have been denied access ever since.

With a broken heart and eyes overflowing I have watched the last war from afar. Operation Cast Lead Israel called it. It was a war that was no war, in which Israel met virtually no resistance, no counterattack worth speaking of. It was just a wild onslaught upon the most helpless population in the world, besieged and jailed, with nowhere to run, not even into the sea. White phosphorous shells scorching living flesh, Flechettes flinging their nails far and wide, manned and unmanned aircraft discharging missiles, disproportionate bombing and shelling. Hundreds of innocents were killed for no other reason other than they were Gazans. The people of Gaza, many of them born to 1948's refugees, who had already suffered one tragedy by Israel's hand, now faced the next chapter in the tragic saga of their lives: an aimless, futile, criminal, superfluous offensive.

I spoke on the phone with my friends there and felt my heart give way. Over 1,300 dead, more than a hundred times the number of Israeli casualties, a horrific ratio rarely paralleled. Over 5,000 wounded, 2,400 buildings destroyed—among them 30 mosques, 121 factories and workshops, and 29 institutions of education. The houses of 350,000 residents were damaged, some beyond recognition. The numbers fail to convey the true dimensions of the horror. And above all there was the new IDF doctrine: a minimum of casualties on our side irrespective of the price. Virtually everything is now fair play.

I was not in Gaza through its last affliction. However, I did watch it very closely from a distance. A few hours after the horrendous attack on the Police College began on Saturday,

December 17, 2008, which killed dozens of young policemen, my first article attacking Cast Lead was printed in *Haaretz*, the paper I work for. I have not stopped speaking out since, like a whistle in the dark, the horrible darkness that has pervaded Israel and the world. Yes, the world too. As the war was raging and the bombs rained down on Gaza, a delegation of EU heads came to Jerusalem to brace the Israeli Prime Minister Ehud Olmert and give him courage. It was a terrible spectacle, a disgraceful parade of the New Europe. None of them took the trouble to visit Gaza, to learn at first hand what atrocities Israel had committed there. This is the same Europe that continues to participate in the blockade of Gaza and the boycott of its government, the only instance of which I am aware of an international boycott of the occupied rather than the occupier.

I think of myself an Israeli patriot. I want to be proud of my country, something that has become increasingly challenging for those Israelis who share my convictions. I also believe that only those who speak up against Israel's policies—who denounce the occupation, the blockade and the war—are the nation's true friends. A real friend does not pick up the bill for an addict's drugs: he packs the friend off to rehab instead. A year has elapsed since hostilities ceased, and Gaza is still in ruins, destitute, jailed and humiliated. The world continues to turn a blind eye. In a glamorous convention in Sharm al-Sheikh, international attendees promised to spend $4.4 billion rebuilding the Strip, but the money hasn't moved from the banks' coffers. It is as if no explicit international commitment was ever expressed. The world looks on impassive.

The world has also read the Goldstone Commission's bold, probing report. Israel rejected it aggressively and bluntly, without even giving it a proper reading. Israel denounced Judge Richard Goldstone, a renowned international jurist—a self-proclaimed Zionist whose daughter spent twelve years in Israel—as an anti-Semite. What he had to say on Rwanda and

Yugoslavia is applauded in Israel; what he wrote about Israel is considered treason. We have a tendency to shoot the messenger and lose the message under the debris. Even his modest demand that Israel investigate what happened was rejected out of hand. Israel should have been grateful to Judge Goldstone for undertaking a duty it has shirked. It should have been the most interested party in the investigation, yet it did not even trouble to begin an inquiry. In the long run Goldstone carries the day: he has laid down the future ethical code for the IDF, regarded by the blind and misguided Israeli public as "the most moral army in the world." Before they set out on another wanton rampage, Israeli generals and politicians will have to pause for thought. A document regarded in my country as vicious has made them understand that they may well have to account personally for any abuse of international law. This is interpreted as the result of pure spite, directed solely at Israel. True, international civil society is critical of Israel, but it has every reason to be. A state pretending to be a democracy, one that presumes to belong to the enlightened Western world and is cashing in on this status, must expect its transgressions and caprices to come under closer critical scrutiny than, for example, the Sudan.

My hope is that this book is a modest contribution to efforts to change the present awful state of affairs. I have been trying to document the Israeli occupation for more than twenty years, during which time the occupation has inexorably tightened its grip. I have sought to record the increasing—and ever more rapid—accumulation of war crimes and human rights abuses committed during that period. It is an exasperating calling to write in Israel what so few want to read. Perhaps this book will prove that notwithstanding what has been said so far, Israel still possesses some dissenting voices.

Lastly, it is my great pleasure to express well-deserved gratitude toward the following. I wish to thank Verso Books and the editor Tom Penn, who courageously ventured to publish the English version of this book. Thanks are due to French publisher La Fabrique and its founding editor, Eric Hazan, for having earlier produced the French edition. My sincere gratitude goes to the exiled Israeli film producer Eyal Sivan for taking on this project, guiding it and selecting the articles that are included herein. I am most profoundly indebted to *Haaretz,* my home for the past twenty-eight years. In the ghastly days of the Gaza offensive my editors stood staunchly by me, with the publisher Amos Schocken and editor in chief Dov Alfon at their head. The constant support I have always enjoyed from *Haaretz*'s editors never wavered. Everything I wrote was printed. All I thought, I was lucky enough to see published. Free expression at its best, uncensored, my work withstood the harshest test and was allowed to thrive through the noise of the guns. I don't take it for granted that articles like mine see publication. At the best of times such subversion is not easily tolerated in Israel; when war is raging, even less so. The pieces in this book were first published against a background of gunfire, at a time when emotional national unity reigned supreme, as it inevitably does in any society in the first days of almost any war. They were printed in the face of chauvinism, militarism, brainwashing, lies, repression and subterfuge. My *Haaretz* editors bravely withstood all this and never faltered, not even in the face of mounting readers' protests and subscription cancellations. This daily newspaper is truly a ray of light in the dark that has descended over Israel.

Having said all this, in both Hebrew and English, I take full and sole responsibility for what you are about to read.

2006

1

A Just Boycott

June 4, 2006

The laugh of fate: The state waging a broad international campaign for a boycott is simultaneously waging a parallel campaign, no less determined, *against* a boycott. A boycott that seriously harms the lives of millions of people is legitimate in the eyes of the state because it is directed against those defined as enemies, while a boycott that is liable to hurt the academic ivory tower is illegitimate in the eyes of the state because it is aimed against itself. This is a moral double standard. Why is the boycott campaign against the Palestinian Authority—including blocking essential economic aid and shunning leaders elected in democratic and legal elections—a permissible measure in Israel's eyes, yet the boycott of Israeli universities is forbidden?

Israel cannot claim that the boycott weapon is illegitimate, because it makes extensive use of this weapon itself, and its victims are suffering under severe conditions of deprivation, from Rafah to Jenin. In the past, Israel called upon the world to boycott Yasser Arafat, and now it is calling for a boycott of the Hamas government—and via this government, all the Palestinians in the territories. And Israel does not regard this as an ethical problem. Tens of thousands of Palestinians have not received their salaries for four months due to the boycott, but when there is a call to boycott Israeli universities, a boycott suddenly becomes an illegitimate weapon.

double standards for the use of boycotts

Those calling for a boycott of Israel are also tainted with a moral double standard. The National Association of Teachers in Further and Higher Education (NATFHE) in Britain, and the Canadian Union of Public Employees in Ontario, which have both decided to boycott Israel, did not act similarly to protest their own countries' war crimes and occupations—the British army in Iraq and the Canadian army in Afghanistan. Nonetheless, the handful of human rights advocates and opponents of the occupation in Israel should thank these two organizations for the step they have taken, despite their flawed double standards.

It would have been preferable if the opponents of the occupation in Israel had not felt the need for the intervention of external groups to help in the struggle. It is not easy to call upon the world to boycott your own country. It would have been better had there been no need for Rachel Corrie, James Miller and Tom Hurndall, bold people of conscience who paid with their lives after standing in front of the destructive bulldozers in Rafah. These young foreigners did the dangerous and vital work that Israelis themselves should have done.

The same is true for the few peace activists who still manage to roam the territories, to protest and offer assistance to the victims of the occupation within the framework of organizations like the International Solidarity Movement (ISM)—which Israel fights, preventing its members from entering its borders. It would be better if Israelis mobilized to fight instead of these activists. But except for a few modest groups, there is no protest in Israel and no real mobilization. Thus, all that remains is to hope for the world's help.

The world can help save Israel from itself in limited ways. In a situation in which the governments of the West effectively support the continuation of the occupation, even if they declare their opposition to it, this role moves to civil organizations. When a group of American attorneys, including Jews, calls for a boycott of the Caterpillar company, whose bulldozers razed complete neighborhoods in Khan Yunis and Rafah, that group should be thanked. The same applies to the boycott of the universities: When an association of British university lecturers boycotts Israeli colleagues who are not prepared even to declare their opposition to the occupation, we should appreciate it. If each group in its field—and perhaps this will someday also include tourism officials, business people, artists and athletes— all boycott Israel, perhaps Israelis will begin to understand, albeit the hard way, that there is a price to pay for the occupation, a price they pay with their pockets and with their status.

The occupation is not just the domain of the government, the army and the security organizations. Everything is tainted: the institutions of justice and law; the physicians who remain silent while medical treatment is prevented in the territories; the teachers who do not protest against the closing of educational institutions and the prevention of free movement of their peers; the journalists who do not report; the writers and artists who remain silent; the architects and engineers who lend a hand to the occupation's enterprises—the settlements and the fence, the barriers and bypass roads; and also the university lecturers, who do nothing for their imprisoned colleagues in the territories, but instead conduct special study programs for the security forces. If all these people were to boycott the occupation, there would be no need for an international boycott.

The world sees a great and ongoing injustice. Should the world remain silent? This is not, of course, the only injustice in the world, nor is it the most terrible. But does that make it any less necessary to act against it?

It is easy to exempt ourselves from our moral responsibility and attribute, as usual, any criticism to anti-Semitism. And there may indeed be some elements of anti-Semitism among those calling for the boycott. But also among them are groups and individuals, including quite a few Jews, for whom Israel is close to their hearts: people who want a just Israel, who see an Israel that occupies and is clearly unjust, and who believe they should do something. We should thank them for this from the bottom of our hearts.

2

Collateral Damage

June 1, 2006

The entire family of Hamdi Aman, a twenty-eight-year-old Palestinian from Gaza who spent his youth in Tel Aviv's Carmel Market, was hit in the assassination of Islamic Jihad operative Mohammed Dahdouh in Gaza a week ago in May of this year.

Aman's seven-year-old son Muhand was killed; Naima, his wife, twenty-seven, was killed; his mother Hanan, forty-six, was killed. His three-and-a-half-year-old daughter Mariya is lying in the pediatric intensive care unit at Sheba Medical Center, Tel Hashomer, permanently paralyzed and on a respirator. Aman is not allowed to be with her.

His youngest son Muaman, two, was lightly wounded in the back by shrapnel, and Aman himself was hit by shrapnel throughout his body. His uncle Nahed, thirty-three, the father of two toddlers, is completely paralyzed and in critical condition at Tel Aviv's Sourasky Medical Center.

The Amans had bought a used Mitsubishi car eleven days before, and they took it for a maiden spin through the Gargash neighborhood in Gaza City. There were eight of them in the car: five adults and three toddlers. Mariya stood dancing on her mother's knees. When they drove down the busy industrial street and passed the home of Palestinian Authority foreign minister Mahmoud al-Zahar, they felt a powerful blow to the left side of the car, exactly when a Magnum van carrying Dahdouh passed them on the left. There was a massive blast, the van with the dead Jihad operative in it was in flames, and Hamdi Aman was faced with the horror that his entire family had been hit.

Israel Air Force chief Major General Eliezer Shkedi said the next day that "we still have to check" what killed the Aman family. The IDF spokesman's office also told *Haaretz* this week, ten days after the assassination, that the IDF is "continuing to investigate in order to check the report that three Palestinians were killed as a result of the attack on Dahdouh's car."

Still have to check

3

"Quiet: We're Shooting"

July 2, 2006

A black flag hangs over the "rolling" operation in Gaza. The more the operation "rolls," the darker the flag becomes. The "summer rains" we are showering on Gaza are not only pointless, they are blatantly illegitimate. It is not legitimate to cut off electricity to 750,000 people. It is not legitimate to call on 20,000 people to run from their homes and turn their towns into ghost towns. It is not legitimate to penetrate Syria's airspace. It is not legitimate to kidnap half of a government and a quarter of a parliament. ~~ISR AS A TERRORIST ORGANIZATION~~

~~A state that takes such steps is no longer distinguishable from a terror organization.~~ The harsher the steps, the more monstrous and stupid they become, the more the moral underpinnings are removed and the stronger the impression that the Israeli government has lost its nerve. Now one must hope that the weekend lull, whether initiated by Egypt or the prime minister—and in any case to the dismay of Channel 2's Roni Daniel and the IDF—will lead to a radical change.

Everything must be done to win Gilad Shalit's release. What we are doing now in Gaza has nothing to do with freeing him. It is a wide-scale act of vengeance, the kind that the IDF and Shin Bet have wanted to conduct for some time, mostly motivated by the deep frustration that the army commanders feel about their impotence against the Qassams and the daring Palestinian guerrilla raid. There's a huge gap between the army unleashing

its frustration and a clever and legitimate operation to free the
kidnapped soldier.

To prevent the army from running as amok as it would like,
a strong and judicious political echelon is required. But facing
off against the frustrated army is Ehud Olmert and Amir Peretz's
amateur regime, weak and hapless. Until the weekend lull, it
appeared that each step proposed by the army and Shin Bet had
been immediately approved for backing. That does not bode
well for the chances of freeing Shalit, let alone for the future
management of the Israeli government, which is being revealed
to be as weak as the Hamas government.

The only wise and restrained voice heard so far was that
of the soldier's father, Noam Shalit, of all people. That noble
man called, at what is clearly his most difficult hour, not for
stridency and not for further damage done to the lives of
soldiers and innocent Palestinians. Against the background of
the IDF's unrestrained actions and the arrogant bragging of the
latest macho spokesmen, Major General Yoav Gallant of the
Southern Command and Major General (Res.) Amos Gilad,
Shalit's father's voice stood out like a cry in the wilderness.

Sending tens of thousands of miserable inhabitants running
from their homes, dozens of kilometers from where Shalit's son
is supposedly hidden, and cutting off the electricity to hundreds
of thousands of others, is certainly not what Shalit meant in his
understated, emotional pleas. It's a shame nobody is listening to
him.

The legitimate basis for the IDF's operation was stripped
away the moment it began. It's no accident that nobody
mentions the day before the attack on the Kerem Shalom
fort, when the IDF kidnapped two civilians, a doctor and his
brother, from their home in Gaza. The difference between us
and them? We kidnapped civilians and they captured a soldier,
which seems to mean that we are a state and they are a terror
organization. How ridiculously pathetic Amos Gilad sounds

when he says that the capture of Shalit was "illegitimate and illegal," unlike when the IDF grabs civilians from their homes. How can a senior official in the defense ministry claim that "the head of the snake" is in Damascus, when the IDF uses the exact same methods?

True, when the IDF and Shin Bet grab civilians from their homes—and they do so often—it is not to murder them later. But sometimes they are killed on the doorsteps of their homes, although it is not necessary, and sometimes they are taken to serve as "bargaining chips," like in Lebanon, and now with the Palestinian legislators. What an uproar there would be if the Palestinians had grabbed half the members of the Israeli government! How would we label them then?

Collective punishment is illegitimate and it does not have a smidgeon of intelligence. Where will the inhabitants of Beit Hanoun run? With typical hardheartedness, the military reporters say they were not "expelled" but that it was "recommended" they leave—for the benefit, of course, of those running for their lives. And what will this inhumane step lead to? Support for the Israeli government? Their enlistment as informants and collaborators for the Shin Bet? Can the miserable farmers of Beit Hanoun and Beit Lahia do anything about the Qassam rocket–launching cells? Did bombing an already destroyed airport do anything to free the soldier, or was it just to decorate the headlines?

Did anyone think about what would have happened if Syrian planes had managed to down one of the Israeli planes that brazenly buzzed their president's palace? Would we have declared war on Syria? Another "legitimate war"? Will the blackout of Gaza bring down the Hamas government or cause the population to rally around it? And even if the Hamas government falls, as Washington wants, what will happen on the day after? These are questions for which nobody has any real answers. As usual here: Quiet, we're shooting. But this time we are not only shooting. We are bombing and shelling, darkening and destroying, imposing a siege and kidnapping like the worst of terrorists, and nobody breaks the silence to ask what the hell for, and according to what right.

4

The Wahbas' Last Meal

July 6, 2006

They'd all sat down to have lunch at home: the mother Fatma, three months pregnant; her daughter Farah, two; her son Khaled, one; Fatma's brother, Dr. Zakariya Ahmed; his daughter-in-law Shayma, nine months pregnant; and the seventy-eight-year-old grandmother. A Wahba family gathering in Khan Yunis in honor of Dr. Ahmed, who'd arrived home six days earlier from Saudi Arabia.

A big boom is heard outside. Fatma hurriedly scoops up the littlest one and tries to escape into an inner room, but another boom follows immediately. This time it is a direct hit. A skilled Israel Air Force pilot fired the second missile and it came right into the dining room through the ceiling. Fatma is killed on the spot by the shrapnel that hits her spine. Her brother, Dr. Ahmed, is also killed. His daughter-in-law miscarries her child; the little girl, Farah, is moderately injured; and the baby of the family, Khaled, is critically injured in the head. A pool of blood collects on the floor. Only the grandmother is unhurt. It will be many minutes before the ambulance arrives. This was the last meal of the Wahba family.

In neighboring Rafah, taxi driver Mohammed Wahba is transporting a family of vacationers to the beach. He hears about the disaster on the radio. His cell phone rings and on the line is his brother Nidal, the father of the family that was hit. "Come quick to get me!" Nidal shouts. The two brothers rush to Nasser Hospital in Khan Yunis, where they see the horror.

Before he became a cab driver, Mohammed worked for nine years at Tel Aviv University as the maintenance man for the Faculty of the Arts, and later for the Faculty of Law. He lived on Einstein Street in Ramat Aviv, and knew many professors by name. It's been ten years now since he was permitted to enter his second city, Tel Aviv. Now he's here, having sat for ten days in a row at the bedside of his toddler nephew, who is in grave condition in the intensive care unit at Dana Children's Hospital next to Ichilov.

Little Khaled is unconscious, paralyzed and on a respirator, wounded in the head by shrapnel from the missile. "I don't know who to blame, if it's the pilot or whoever gave the order to attack. Who bears the responsibility?" Mohammed asks in excellent Hebrew. The targeted assassination, which was aimed at a vehicle carrying members of the Popular Resistance Committees that was driving down the street, and fell instead right on a family in the middle of their lunch, he calls "an accident."

His brother Nidal, now a widower, calls all the time from Khan Yunis to ask how his unconscious son is doing. The Coordination and Liaison Office has already called to say the child will have to be brought back to Gaza, due to lack of funds to keep him hospitalized in Israel. The father and uncle are terribly worried about what that will mean. This week, Ibrahim Habib of Physicians for Human Rights tried to prevent the child from being returned to Gaza.

The Wahbas had tried for years to have a child. They underwent fertility treatment in Gaza and finally, two and a half years ago, their daughter Farah was born. Khaled was born a year later. Nidal is a metallurgical engineer who studied in Germany and works as a supervisor in the professional schools in Gaza, and Fatma was a teacher. He is forty, she was thirty-six. Their house is located under the Welcome to Khan Yunis sign at the northern entrance to the city, on the highway between Gaza and Rafah. Israeli tanks will probably be rolling down the road before long, but two weeks ago on Wednesday, all was quiet in the city as the family sat down to a special lunch to celebrate Dr. Ahmed's return from Saudi Arabia.

Mohammed was driving his cab through the streets of Rafah. Thirty-five years old, he was born in Rafah's Yavneh refugee camp and at the age of fourteen came to Tel Aviv University, where he worked in the Student Association cafeteria. When he became a maintenance man he lived in a rented room in the apartment of an elderly man named Yaakov Kleiner, on Einstein Street. He remembers the cigars favored by faculty dean Arnon Zuckerman and the times of the classes given by guest lecturers Haim Yavin (Thursday afternoon) and Rafik Halabi; he remembers student Zvika Hadar and theater professors David Zinder, Tom Levy and Hana Taragan. He especially enjoyed the International Student Film Festival the department held every year. "It was so nice there," he says. He remembers the security people there, too, though not their names. And Livio Carmeli and his film archive.

From the Gilman Building, Mohammed remembers Professor Israel Gershoni, and from the Faculty of Law, he remembers professors Eliezer Lederman, the late Menashe Shava, Kenneth Mann and Shlomo Shoham. All were very friendly to him. It was the best time of his life. In 1994, when entry into Israel was limited to married men with families and Mohammed was still single, this nice period of his life came to an end. There was just one more time that he was able to enter Israel, and then he went directly to the Ramat Aviv campus. That was in 1997, right after his marriage, and he enjoyed a day full of memories. He hadn't been back since, until now, when he finds himself waiting by the door of the pediatric intensive care unit. Professor Lederman has promised to come visit him.

It was the longest day of the year, June 21. At about 4:30 in the afternoon Mohammed Wahba was driving a family to the Rafah beach, not far from the ruins of Rafiah Yam, when a report came on the radio about another targeted assassination attempt. At first, the announcer said it was the "Barbawi family" that was hurt, and Mohammed was somewhat relieved: He didn't know them. But later, on his way back from the sea, the report was that a pregnant thirty-six-year-old teacher named Fatma had been killed.

His heart skipped a beat. There was only one pregnant teacher named Fatma in Khan Yunis, he thought—his sister-in-law. And then his brother Nidal called: "Did you listen to the news?" "No, I didn't hear it," he lied, to avoid scaring his brother. Then his brother-in-law, who works at Nasser Hospital, also called, confirming Mohammed's worst fears. It had been his brother's family that had been hurt by the missile. Mohammed picked up Nidal from the center of Rafah, and together they drove to the hospital in Khan Yunis. Khaled was in critical condition, with extensive bleeding in the brain. Fatma and Dr. Ahmed were already dead. Farah had been wounded in the back by shrapnel. Khaled was immediately taken to Shifa Hospital in Gaza, where surgeons operated on his head. The grandmother told them afterward that she'd tried to lift Khaled off the floor, and that's when she'd seen that her daughter and son had been killed.

The intervention of a family friend—an American who had lived in the Shabura camp in Rafah for years and called from America—led to Khaled being transferred to the hospital in Tel Aviv. The Light to the Nations organization, an American foundation, promised to pay for the treatment. Not the IDF, not the air force, not the Defense Ministry.

On Sunday, three days after the event, Khaled was transferred to a hospital in Israel, accompanied by Mohammed. This week his condition was described as close to hopeless, and the family was told that he'd have to be taken back to Gaza. The doctors told Mohammed that "the situation is out of our hands." A spokeswoman for Ichilov Hospital confirmed that Khaled's condition is critical as a result of the injury to his head. At the beginning of the week, the defense minister's adviser had not replied to the request from Physicians for Human Rights that Khaled not be returned to Gaza. Mohammed is convinced that bringing the child back to Gaza will seal his fate.

According to the IDF spokesman, this week: "The IDF attack on June 21 was directed against a terror cell that was on its way to perpetrate a terror attack. The attack was carried out shortly after two previous aerial assaults in which, for various reasons, uninvolved Palestinian civilians were hurt. In this assault, lessons learned from previous assaults were already implemented, as far as going to greater lengths to ensure that no civilians are within the risk area.

"However, for reasons that are not yet entirely clear, one of the two missiles that were fired deviated from the target at which it was directed. The result of this deviation was a strike on a residential building located dozens of meters from the target, a building occupied by the Palestinian civilians who were harmed.

"It should be noted that the method used by the IDF in performing such missions has been proven over the years as accurate and cautious, and in the majority of cases enables the IDF to act against terror organizations and activists who deliberately take shelter among and act from within a civilian population, under the cover of a population that is not involved in its activities.

"It should be emphasized that in a situation in which it is clearly seen that there is a risk to the population that is located near the target, the planned assault is then canceled, even when it is clearly known that the object of the attack constitutes a serious threat. Unfortunately, in ongoing combat of this sort,

refuses to take blame

accidents happen and innocent civilians are harmed. We regret this, yet the responsibility lies entirely with the terror organizations and the leadership of the Palestinian Authority which does nothing to stop them.

"When the investigation of the incident is completed, the findings will be presented to the chief of staff."

"They always said the helicopters were the smartest weapons. Suddenly it's the dumbest weapon," says Mohammed, bleary-eyed. "It's happened to other families, too. I don't know when it will stop. If it keeps on like this, I don't know how it will end. Who can put a stop to it? Only the two peoples. They're the ones with the pain and the suffering. Not the governments or the leaders. Only the peoples can put an end to this business. The Israelis and the Palestinians. Olmert's son doesn't serve in the army, and Haniyeh's son doesn't go around with a rifle opposing the occupation."

How does it feel to be back in Tel Aviv?

"It feels quiet and safe here. Not like in Gaza. There, you feel unsafe all the time. Don't forget I'm a cab driver. Maybe they'll attack the car in front of me or behind me? It's like how I heard it was for you during the time of all the terror attacks."

Mohammed's brother Nidal is in a bad state. He lives on coffee and cigarettes and suffers attacks of fury and anxiety. "What happened, happened, and who's gone is gone, but what about this boy?" he said to his brother this week on the phone. Every half-hour Mohammed goes to the intensive care room to check on his nephew's condition. Khaled lies there unconscious, stitches crisscrossing his tiny head and tubes sticking out of his mouth and body. Mohammed says Khaled has actually moved a little bit in the past couple of days.

5

Who Started It?

July 9, 2006

"We left Gaza and they are firing Qassams"—there is no more precise a formulation of the prevailing view about the current round of the conflict. "They started it" will be the routine response to anyone who tries to argue, for example, that a few hours before the first Qassam fell on the school in Ashkelon, causing no damage, Israel sowed destruction at the Islamic University in Gaza.

Israel is causing electricity blackouts; laying sieges; bombing and shelling; assassinating and imprisoning; killing and wounding civilians, including children and babies, in horrifying numbers—but "they started it."

They are also "breaking the rules" laid down by Israel: We are allowed to bomb anything we want and they are not allowed to launch Qassams. When they fire a Qassam at Ashkelon, that's an "escalation of the conflict," but when we bomb a university and a school, it's perfectly all right. Why? Because they started it. That's why the majority thinks that all the justice is on our side. Like in a schoolyard fight, Israel's assurance that they started it is the winning moral argument to justify every injustice.

So, who really did start it? And has Israel "left Gaza"?

Only partially, and in a distorted manner. The disengagement plan, which was labeled with fancy phrases like "partition" and "an end to the occupation," did result in the dismantling of settlements and the Israel Defense Forces' departure from Gaza, but it did almost nothing to change the living conditions for the residents of the Strip. Gaza is still a prison, and its inhabitants are still doomed to live in poverty and oppression. Israel closes them off from the sea, the air and land, except for a limited safety valve at the Rafah crossing. Residents cannot visit their relatives in the West Bank or look for work in Israel, upon which the Gazan economy has been dependent for some forty years. Sometimes goods can be transported, sometimes not. Gaza has no chance of escaping its poverty under these conditions. Nobody will invest in it, nobody can develop it, nobody can feel free in it. Israel locked the cage, threw away the keys and left the residents to their bitter fate. Now, less than a year after the disengagement, Israel is going back, with violence and force.

What could otherwise have been expected? That Israel would unilaterally withdraw, brutally and outrageously ignoring the Palestinians and their needs, and that the Palestinians would silently bear their bitter fate and not try to fight for their liberty, livelihood and dignity? We promised a safe passage to the West Bank and didn't keep the promise. We promised to free prisoners and didn't keep the promise. We supported democratic elections and then boycotted the legally elected leadership, confiscated funds that belong to it and declared war on it. We could have withdrawn from Gaza through negotiations and coordination, while strengthening the existing Palestinian leadership, but we refused to do so. And now we complain about "a lack of leadership"? We did everything we could to undermine their society and leadership, making as sure as possible that the disengagement would not be a new chapter in our relationship with the neighboring nation, and now we are amazed by the violence and hatred that we sowed with our own hands.

What would have happened if the Palestinians had not fired Qassams? Would Israel have lifted the economic siege that it imposed on Gaza? Would it open the border to Palestinian laborers? Free prisoners? Meet with the elected leadership and conduct negotiations? Encourage investment in Gaza? Nonsense. If the Gazans were sitting quietly, as Israel expects them to do, their case would disappear from the agenda—here and around the world. Israel would continue with the convergence, which is solely meant to serve our goals, ignoring their needs. Nobody would have given any thought to the fate of the people of Gaza if they had not behaved violently. That is a very bitter truth, but the first twenty years of the occupation passed quietly and we did not lift a finger to end it.

Instead, under cover of the quiet, we built the enormous, criminal settlement enterprise. With our own hands, we are now once again pushing the Palestinians into using what petty arms they have; and in response, we employ nearly the entire enormous arsenal at our disposal, and continue to complain that "they started it!"

We started it. We started it with the occupation, and we are duty-bound to end it—a real and complete ending. We started the violence. There is no violence worse than the violence of the occupier, using force on an entire nation, so the question about who fired first is therefore an evasion meant to distort the picture. After Oslo, too, there were those who claimed that "we left the territories," with a similar mixture of blindness and lies.

Gaza is in serious trouble, ruled by death, horror and daily difficulties, far from the eyes and hearts of Israelis. We are only shown the Qassams. We only see the Qassams. The West Bank is still under the boot of occupation, the settlements are flourishing, and every hand limply extended for an agreement, including that of Ismail Haniyeh, is immediately rejected. And after all this, if someone still has second thoughts, the winning answer is promptly delivered: "They started it. They started it and justice is on our side." But the fact is that they did not start it, and justice is not with us.

6

Gaza's Darkness

September 3, 2006

Gaza has been reoccupied. The world must know this, and Israelis must know it, too. It is in its worst condition ever. Since the abduction of Gilad Shalit, and more so since the outbreak of the Lebanon war, the Israel Defense Forces has been rampaging through Gaza—there's no other word to describe it—killing and demolishing, bombing and shelling indiscriminately.

Nobody thinks about setting up a commission of inquiry; the issue isn't even on the agenda. Nobody asks why it is being done and who decided to do it. But under the cover of the darkness of the Lebanon war, the IDF returned to its old practices in Gaza as if there had been no disengagement. So it must be said forthrightly: The disengagement is dead. Aside from the settlements that remain piles of rubble, nothing is left of the disengagement and its promises. How contemptible all the sublime and nonsensical talk about "the end of the occupation" and "partitioning the land" now appears. Gaza is occupied, and with greater brutality than before. The fact that it is more convenient for the occupier to control it from outside has nothing to do with the intolerable living conditions of the occupied.

In large parts of Gaza nowadays, there is no electricity. Israel bombed the only power station there, and more than half the electricity supply will be cut off for at least another year. Since there is no electricity, supplying homes with water is nearly impossible. Gaza is filthier and smellier than ever. Because of the embargo Israel and the world have imposed on the elected authority, no salaries are being paid and the street cleaners have been on strike for weeks. Piles of garbage and clouds of stink strangle the coastal strip, turning it into Calcutta.

More than ever, Gaza is also like a prison. The Erez crossing is empty, the Karni and Rafah crossings have been open only a few days over the last two months. Some 15,000 people waited for two months to enter Egypt, and some are still waiting, including many who are ailing and wounded. Another 5,000 waited on the other side to return to their homes. Some died during the wait. One must see the scenes at Rafah to understand how profound a human tragedy is taking place. A crossing that was not supposed to have an Israeli presence continues to be Israel's means to pressure 1.5 million inhabitants. This is disgraceful and shocking collective punishment. The United States and Europe, whose police are at the Rafah crossing, also bear responsibility for the situation.

Gaza is also poorer and hungrier than ever before. There is nearly no merchandise moving in and out, fishing is banned, the tens of thousands of PA workers receive no salaries, and the possibility of working in Israel is out of the question.

And we still haven't mentioned the death, destruction and horror. In the last two months, Israel killed 224 Palestinians, 62 of them children and 25 of them women. It bombed and assassinated, destroyed and shelled, and no one stopped it. No Qassam cell or smuggling tunnel justifies such wide-scale killing. A day doesn't go by without deaths, most of them innocent civilians.

Where are the days when there was still a debate in Israel about the assassinations? Today, Israel drops innumerable missiles, shells and bombs on houses and kills entire families on its way to another assassination. Hospitals are collapsing, with more than 900 people undergoing treatment. Last week at Shifa Hospital, the only such facility in Gaza that might be worthy of being called a hospital, I saw heartrending scenes: children who had lost limbs, on respirators, paralyzed, crippled for the rest of their lives.

Entire families have been killed in their sleep or while riding on donkeys or working in fields. Frightened children, traumatized by what they have seen, huddle in their homes with a horror in their eyes that is difficult to describe in words. A journalist from Spain who spent time in Gaza recently, a veteran of war and disaster zones around the world, said he had never been exposed to scenes as horrific as the ones he had seen and documented over the last two months.

It is difficult to determine who decided on all of this. It is doubtful the ministers are aware of the reality in Gaza. They are responsible for it, starting with the bad decision on the embargo, through the bombing of Gaza's bridges and power station and the mass assassinations. Israel is responsible, once again, for all that happens in Gaza.

The events in Gaza expose the great fraud of Kadima: It came to power on the coattails of the virtual success of the disengagement, which is now going up in flames, and it promised convergence, a promise that the prime minister has already rescinded. Those who think Kadima is a centrist party should now know it is nothing other than another rightist occupation party. The same is true of Labor. Defense Minister Amir Peretz is responsible for what is happening in Gaza no less than the prime minister, and Peretz's hands are as blood-soaked as Olmert's. He can never present himself as a "man of peace" again. The ground invasions every week, each time somewhere else, the kill-and-destroy operations from the sea, air and land are all given names that whitewash the reality, like "Summer Rains" or "Locked Kindergarten." No security excuse can explain the cycle of madness, and no civic argument can excuse the outrageous silence of us all. Gilad Shalit will not be released and the Qassams will not cease. On the contrary, there is a horror taking place in Gaza, and while it might prevent a few terror attacks in the short run, it is bound to give birth to much more murderous terror. Israel will then say, with its self-righteousness: "But we returned Gaza to them!"

2007

7

The Little Ahmadinejads

June 8, 2007

Ram Caspi has written an article. From the heights of his apartment in Tel Aviv's David Towers, the prominent lawyer has suggested strangulating the Gaza Strip. In the financial daily *Globes* of May 25, he called for "neither a land incursion nor an aerial attack, but the creation of a noose . . . From the moment that rocket number eight is fired, the government of Israel will act to cut Gaza off from the essential infrastructure systems of fuel, water, electricity and telephones, and will prevent others from providing these utilities to Gaza."

In other words: to cut 1.5 million people off from the sources of life.

Caspi is a successful attorney, who comes and goes in the tabernacles of justice and rule, a man who moves about in the highest reaches of Israeli society. Not a hair on his head has been mussed as a result of his satanic proposal. This man of the law who advocates for the violation of international law has not been chastised. No one has shunned him in the wake of his words. The season for racism, collective punishment and verbal violence is at its height. What was once the reserve of nutcases on the right, the talk-backers and the loony listeners to the call-in radio programs, is now politically correct, in the heart of the consensus, the *dernier cri* in the violent and overheated Israeli discourse.

Caspi is not alone. Satan is no longer to be found only in Tehran—he is alive and kicking here in our midst. Israel is being inundated by a murky stream of little blue-and-white Ahmadinejads. If the president of Iran proposes to destroy Israel, they, who are smaller than he, are proposing only to "eradicate" villages, to "flatten" them, to starve entire populations and in fact to kill them.

There is no difference, in principle or morality, between the Iranian original and his Israeli imitators. The racist and bullying philosophy of Minister of Strategic Affairs Avigdor Lieberman and his ilk has unleashed its malignant tentacles into the heart of society. Meir Kahane, who made proposals more moderate than these, found himself shunned; Caspi continues to advise the top people in the country on legal matters.

This ugly and appalling phenomenon had its beginnings last summer, during the Second Lebanon War. "We are allowed to have another Kfar Kana, we are allowed to destroy everything," said the justice minister at the time, Haim Ramon, the man who was in charge of maintaining the law. Trade and Industry Minister Eli Yishai, a representative of a religious party that has a "spiritual" leadership, did not lag behind him—he proposed targeting infrastructure in Lebanon and "flattening" villages.

These two calls to commit war crimes did not emerge from the mouths of representatives of the extreme right. Ramon and Yishai have remained legitimate spokesmen. Nor did the generals keep quiet: "Grind Lebanon. Turn it into a museum of the incubation of terror," proposed a former chief of Northern Command headquarters, Brigadier General (Res.) Rafi Noy, a desired interviewee in the studios.

The Qassams on Sderot presaged the disgusting continuation, this time in poetry as well. "If not the roof beams, destroy the foundations . . . Attack Lebanon and also Gaza with plows and with salt, destroy them so no inhabitant remains. Transform them into barren desert, piles of rubble . . . kill them, spill their blood, frighten the living," wrote poet Ilan Scheinfeld, who has recently published a novel for which no one has called a boycott.

Former chief rabbi Mordechai Eliyahu has called for returning fire on homes; Minister of Pensioner Affairs Rafi Eitan has proposed that Israel manufacture a domestic version of the Qassam and launch it on Gaza; Public Security Minister Avi Dichter has said that targeted assassinations are not enough; his successor at the Shin Bet security service, Yuval Diskin, has complained that "in Beit Lahia and in Beit Hanoun they are living in tranquility"; our old acquaintance Lieberman has proposed a hit on the quarter where Gaza City's well-off reside for every hit on Sderot; Major General (Res.) Amiram Levin has called for dividing the Gaza Strip into squares, and for destroying one after every Qassam; former justice minister Yosef Lapid supported this proposal; former chief of staff Moshe Ya'alon, the progenitor of the theory of "consciousness-searing," has proposed "cleansing the territory"; Sderot Mayor Eli Moyal has said that he prefers "a dead child in Gaza to a dead child in Sderot"; and a bereaved father from the Second Lebanon War, Ami Schreier, has called for the wiping out of a neighborhood in Gaza, with advance warning of three hours, for every Qassam.

Not one of them has been castigated for his words, not one of them shunned. *— no one questioned for abhorrent ideas*
This is what we look like. This is our moral portrait.

8

A War on Children

September 2, 2007

Again children. Five children killed in Gaza in eight days. The public indifference to their killing—the last three, for example, were accorded only a short item on the margins of page 11 in *Yedioth Ahronoth*, a sickening matter in itself—cannot blur the fact that the IDF is waging a war against children. A year ago, a fifth of those killed in the "Summer Rain" operation in Gaza were children; during the past two weeks, children comprised a quarter of the twenty-one killed. If, heaven forbid, children are hurt in Sderot, we will have to remember this before we begin raising hell.

The IDF explains that the Palestinians make a practice of sending children to collect the Qassam launchers. However, in this case, the children killed were not collecting launchers. The first two were killed while collecting carob fruit, and the next three—according to the IDF's own investigation—were playing tag. But even if we accept the IDF's claim that there is a general trend of sending children to collect launchers (which has not been proven), that should have brought about an immediate halt to firing at launcher collectors.

But the IDF does not care whether its victims are liable to be children. The fact is that it shoots at figures it considers suspicious, with full knowledge—according to its own contention—that they are liable to be children. Therefore, an IDF that fires at launcher collectors is an army that kills children, without

Shooting indiscriminately @ children

have me / no ethical considerations

taking any steps to avoid doing so. This is not a series of unfortunate mistakes, as it is being portrayed, but rather a reflection the army's contempt for the lives of Palestinian children and its terrifying indifference to their fate.

A society that holds ethical considerations in high regard would at least ask itself: Is it permissible to shoot at anyone who is approaching the launchers, even if we know that some of these people may be small children lacking in judgment, and thus not punishable? Or are we lifting all restraints on our war operations? Even if we accept the IDF's claims that its sophisticated vision devices cannot distinguish between a ten-year-old boy and an adult, the IDF cannot evade its responsibility for this criminal action. Even if we accept the completely distorted assumption that anyone who goes near the launchers is subject to death, the fact that children are involved should have changed the rules. Add to this the fact that firing at launcher collectors has not halted the Qassams, or even reduced their number, and you arrive at another chilling conclusion: The IDF shoots at children to wreak vengeance and punish.

No child in Sderot is more secure as a result of this killing. On the contrary.

Anyone who takes an honest look at the progression of events during the past two months will discover that the Qassams have a context: They are almost always fired after an IDF assassination operation, and there have been many of these. The question of who started it is not a childish question in this context. The IDF has returned to liquidations, and in a big way. And in their wake there has been an increase in Qassam firings.

That is the truth, and the IDF is hiding it from us. When Gabi Ashkenazi and Ehud Barak assumed their positions, the reins were loosened. If Barak were a representative of the political right, perhaps a public outcry would have already been sounded against the IDF's wild actions in Gaza. But everything is permitted by Barak, and even the fact that the victims are children does not matter—not to him, and not to the Israeli public.

Yes, the children of Gaza gather around the Qassams. It is practically the only diversion they have in their lives. It is their amusement park. Those who arrogantly preach that the parents should "watch over them" have never visited Beit Hanoun. There is nothing there except filthy alleys and meager homes. Even if it is true that those launching the Qassams are taking advantage of these miserable children (which has yet to be proven), this should not shape our moral portrait. Yes, it is permissible to exercise restraint and caution. Yes, it is not always necessary to respond, especially when the response ends up killing children.

The way to stop the firing of Qassams is not through indiscriminate killing. Every launcher can be replaced. The start of the school year bodes ill, both for us and for them. Anyone who truly seeks to stop the firing of Qassams should strive to reach a cease-fire agreement with the current government in Gaza. That is the only way, and it is possible. The liquidations, the shelling and the killing of children will work in exactly the opposite direction from what is intended. In the meantime, look what is happening to us and to our army.

9

The Children of 5767

September 27, 2009

It was a pretty quiet year, relatively speaking. Only 457 Palestinians and 10 Israelis were killed, according to the human rights organization B'Tselem, including the victims of Qassam rockets. That's fewer casualties than in many previous years. However, it was still a terrible year: ninety-two Palestinian children were killed (fortunately, not a single Israeli child was killed by Palestinians, despite the Qassams). One-fifth of the Palestinians killed were children and teens—a disproportionate, almost unprecedented number. This is the Jewish year 5767. Almost 100 children, who were alive and playing last New Year's, didn't survive to see this one.

One year. Close to 8,000 kilometers were covered in the newspaper's small, armored Rover—not including the hundreds of kilometers in the old yellow Mercedes taxi belonging to Munir and Sa'id, our dedicated drivers in Gaza. This is how we celebrated the fortieth anniversary of the occupation. No one can argue anymore that it's only a temporary, passing phenomenon. Israel is the occupation. The occupation is Israel. *defines its struggle*

We set out each week in the footsteps of the fighters, in the West Bank and the Gaza Strip, trying to document the deeds of Israel Defense Forces soldiers, Border Police officers, Shin Bet security service investigators and Civil Administration personnel—the mighty occupation army that has left horrific killing and destruction in its wake, this year as every year, for four decades.

And this was the year of the children that were killed. We didn't get to all of their homes, only to some; homes of bereavement where parents weep bitterly over their lost children, who had been doing nothing worse than climbing a fig tree in the yard, or sitting on a bench in the street, or preparing for an exam, or traveling home from school, or sleeping peacefully in the false security of their homes.

A few of the children also threw a rock at an armored vehicle or touched a forbidden fence. All came under live fire, some of which was deliberately aimed at them, cutting them down in their youth. From Mohammed (al-Zakh) to Mahmoud (al-Qarinawi), from the boy who was buried twice in Gaza to the boy who was buried in Israel. Here are the stories of the children of 5767.

The first of them was buried twice. Abdullah al-Zakh identified half of the body of his son Mahmoud, in the morgue refrigerator of Shifa Hospital in Gaza, by the boy's belt and the socks on his feet. This was shortly before last Rosh Hashanah. The next day, when the Israel Defense Forces "successfully" completed Operation Locked Kindergarten, as it was called, and withdrew from Sajiyeh in Gaza—leaving behind twenty-two dead and a neighborhood razed—the bereaved father found the remaining parts of the boy's body and brought them for a belated burial. Mahmoud was fourteen when he died. He was killed three days before the start of the school year. Thus we ushered in Rosh Hashanah 5767.

In Shifa we saw children whose legs had been amputated, children who were paralyzed or on respirators. Operation Locked Kindergarten and Operation Summer Rains. Remember? Five children were killed in the first operation, the one with the dreadful name. For a week, the people of Sajiyeh lived in fear the likes of which Sderot residents have never experienced—not to belittle their anxiety.

The day after Rosh Hashanah we traveled to Rafah. Dam Hamad, fourteen, had been killed in her sleep, in her mother's arms, by an Israeli rocket strike that sent a concrete pillar crashing down on her head. She was the only daughter of her paralyzed mother, her whole world. In the family's impoverished home in the Brazil neighborhood at the edge of Rafah, we met the mother, who lay in a heap in bed: everything she had in the world was gone. Outside, I remarked to the French television reporter who accompanied me that this was one of those moments when I felt ashamed to be an Israeli. The next day he called and said: "They didn't broadcast what you said, for fear of the Jewish viewers in France."

Soon afterward we went back to Jerusalem to visit Maria Aman, the amazing little girl from Gaza who lost nearly everyone in her life, including her mother, to a missile strike gone awry that wiped out her innocent family. Her devoted father Hamdi remains by her side. For a year and a half, she has been cared for at the wonderful Alyn Hospital, where she has learned to feed a parrot with her mouth and to operate her wheelchair using her chin. All her limbs are paralyzed. She is connected day and night to a respirator. Still, she is a cheerful and neatly groomed child whose father fears the day they might be sent back to Gaza. For now, they remain in Israel. Many Israelis have devoted themselves to Maria and come to visit her regularly. A few weeks ago, broadcast journalist Leah Lior took Maria in her car to see the sea in Tel Aviv. It was a Saturday night, and the area was crowded with people out for a good time, but the girl in the wheelchair attracted attention. Some people recognized her and stopped to say hello and wish her well. Who knows? Maybe the pilot who fired the missile at the Amans' car happened to be passing by, too.

Not everyone has been fortunate enough to receive the treatment that Maria has had. In mid-November, a few days after the

bombardment of Beit Hanoun—remember that?—we arrived
in the battered and bleeding town: eleven shells dropped on a
densely packed town, twenty-two killed in a moment. Islam,
fourteen, was dressed in black, grieving for eight relatives who
had been killed, including her mother and grandmother. Those
disabled by this bombardment didn't get to go to Alyn.

Two days before the shelling of Beit Hanoun, our forces
also fired a missile that hit the minibus transporting children to
the Indira Gandhi kindergarten in Beit Lahia. Two children,
passersby, were killed on the spot. The teacher, Najweh Khalif,
died a few days later. She was wounded in clear view of her
twenty small pupils, who were sitting in the minibus. After her
death, the children drew a picture: a row of children lying bleeding, their teacher in the front, and an Israeli plane bombing them.

At the Indira Gandhi kindergarten, we had to bid goodbye
to Gaza, too: Since then, we haven't been able to cross into the
Strip.

But the children have come to us. In November, thirty-one
children were killed in Gaza. One of them, Ayman al-Mahdi,
died in Sheba Medical Center at Tel Hashomer, where he had
been rushed in grave condition. Only his uncle was permitted
to stay with him during his final days. A fifth-grader, Ayman
had been sitting with friends on a bench on a street in Jabalya,
right by his school, when a bullet fired from a tank struck him
down. He was just ten years old.

IDF troops killed children in the West Bank, too. Jamil Jabaji,
a fourteen-year-old boy who tended horses in the new Askar
refugee camp, was shot in the head and killed last December.
He and his friends were throwing rocks at the armored vehicle that passed by the camp, located near Nablus. The driver
provoked the children, slowing down and speeding up, slowing
down and speeding up, until finally a soldier got out, aimed his
gun at the boy's head and fired. Jamil's horses were left in their
stable, and his family was left to mourn.

And what did sixteen-year-old Taha al-Jawi do to get himself killed? The IDF claimed that he tried to sabotage the barbed-wire fence surrounding the abandoned Atarot Airport; his friends said he was just playing soccer and had gone after the ball. Whatever the circumstances, the response from the soldiers was quick and decisive: a bullet in the leg that caused Taha to bleed to death, lying in a muddy ditch by the side of the road. Live fire directed at unarmed children who weren't endangering anyone, with no prior warning. Not a word of regret, not a word of condemnation from the IDF spokesman when we asked for a comment.

Abir Aramin was even younger; she was just eleven. The daughter of an activist in the Combatants for Peace organization, in January she left her school in Anata and was on the way to buy candy in a little shop when she was fired upon from a Border Police vehicle. Her father Bassam told us, with bloodshot eyes and in a strangled voice: "I told myself that I don't want to take revenge. Revenge will be for this 'hero,' who was so 'threatened' by my daughter that he shot and killed her, to stand trial for it." But just a few days ago the authorities announced that the case was being closed: The Border Police apparently acted appropriately.

the border police had "acted appropriately"

"I'm not going to exploit my daughter's blood for political purposes," the grieving father, who has many Israeli friends, also told us. "This is a human outcry. I'm not going to lose my mind just because I lost my heart."

In Nablus, we documented the use of children as human shields—the use of the so-called "neighbor procedure"—involving an eleven-year-old girl, a twelve-year-old boy and a fifteen-year-old boy. So what if the High Court of Justice has outlawed it? We also recorded the story of the death of baby Khaled, whose parents, Sana and Daoud Fakih, tried to rush him to the hospital in the middle of the night, a time when Palestinian babies apparently mustn't get sick: The baby died at the checkpoint.

In Kafr al-Shuhada (the "martyrs' village"), south of Jenin, in
March, fifteen-year-old Ahmed Asasa was fleeing from soldiers
who had entered the village when a sniper's bullet caught him
in the neck.

Bushra Bargis hadn't even left her home. In late April she was
studying for a big test, notebooks in hand, pacing around her
room in the Jenin refugee camp in the early evening, when a
sniper shot her in the forehead from quite far away. Her bloodstained notebooks bear witness to her final moments.

And what about the unborn babies? They weren't safe either.
A bullet in the back of Maha Qatuni—who was seven months
pregnant and got up during the night to protect her children in
their home—struck her fetus in the womb, shattering its head.
The wounded mother lay in the Rafidiya Hospital in Nablus,
hooked up to numerous tubes. She was going to name the baby
Daoud. Does killing a fetus count as murder? And how "old"
was the deceased? He was certainly the youngest of the many
children Israel has killed in the past year.

Happy New Year.

10

Puppet Leader

September 23, 2007

Mahmoud Abbas has to stay home. As things stand right now, he must not go to Washington. Even his meetings with Ehud Olmert are gradually turning into a disgrace and have become a humiliation for his people. Nothing good will come of them. It has become impossible to bear the spectacle of the Palestinian leader's jolly visits in Jerusalem, kissing the cheek of the wife of the very prime minister who is meanwhile threatening to blockade 1.5 million of his people, condemning them to darkness and hunger.

If Abu Mazen were a genuine national leader instead of a petty retailer, he would refuse to participate in the summit, and any other meetings, until the blockade of Gaza is lifted. If he were a man of truly historic stature, he would add that no conference can be held without Ismail Haniyeh, another crucial Palestinian representative. And if Israel really wanted peace, not only an "agreement of principles" with a puppet leader that will lead nowhere, it should respect Abbas's demand. Israel should aspire for Abu Mazen to be considered a leader in the eyes of his people; not a marionette whose strings are pulled by Israel and the United States, and who is affected by other short-term power plays.

Right now power rests with the powerless Abu Mazen. Since Washington—and perhaps Jerusalem as well—badly want the photo-op otherwise known as a "peace summit" to show off an "achievement," Abu Mazen could and should threaten to boycott the meeting to try and force some achievement on behalf of his people. Palestinians live in Gaza, too—an area controlled by Hamas, which Abu Mazen so loathes: He cannot continue to ignore the inhumane conditions in which Gazans live, caged in by Israel.

But the impression Abu Mazen makes is that he's no more than a political survivor. He's participating in the American–Israeli masked ball not because of naïveté or weakness—for him, Gaza is just as much "hostile territory" as Israel is. Therefore, he shares a shameful common interest with Israel, which will do neither side any good. Judging by his behavior, Abu Mazen not only doesn't object to what Israel is doing in Gaza, he may even agree with the twisted doctrine arguing that cruel pressure will subdue Hamas and return the people to Fatah's embrace. In so doing, Abu Mazen proves that he's no "downy chick," as Ariel Sharon once put it, but a cynical rooster who cares little for the welfare of his people.

A genuine peace conference should involve all the hawks. Peace is forged between bitter enemies. The question of whether Saudi Arabia will take part in the summit or not is futile unless it includes real Palestinian representation. At most, Abu Mazen represents only half of his people and could achieve, at best, half an agreement, which wouldn't survive anyhow, given Hamas's strong opposition. It is in the interests of all parties involved, including Abu Mazen, to drag Hamas to the negotiation table. A peace conference without Hamas or Syria is a joke. But the short-sighted coalition of the royal triumvirate, Jerusalem-Washington-Ramallah, is trying to promote a false vision of "peace talks" without the decisive partners, while the world is busy applauding this illusion.

Obviously, it is hard to expect that Abu Mazen will rise above his narrow interests and call for an invitation to be issued to Hamas, the party that was democratically elected to lead the Palestinian government. But the least one could hope for from the person with the lofty title of President of the Palestinian Authority is to strive for the greater good of all his people, especially given the extent of their distress. But instead of acting to bring about a cessation of hostilities and opening Gaza to the world, the triumvirate is busy formulating yet another position paper that won't be worth the paper it's written on, and that will soon find itself in the garbage bin of history, along with its predecessors. It will only serve to impose increasingly cruel hardships on the people of Gaza. Abu Mazen must not participate in this farce.

11

Wanted: Israeli Journalists in Gaza

October 14, 2007

Nearly a year has passed since we traveled together to the Indira Gandhi Kindergarten. We traveled to this playground, on the outskirts of Beit Lahia, with our dedicated Gazan taxi drivers, Munir and Sa'id, to document the killing of kindergarten teacher Najweh Khalif in front of her children by an errant tank shell that missed the kindergarten's minibus by only several meters. We have not been able to return to Gaza since.

The Gaza Strip has been completely closed to Israeli journalists for nearly a year. The Israel Defense Forces and Shin Bet security service decided this because it is dangerous in Gaza. An Israeli journalist can travel to Syria, Iraq and Saudi Arabia, but not to Gaza. An Israeli journalist can travel to Sinai, where it is also said to be dangerous. The West Bank is still open to journalists, where it is clearly dangerous. But a complete blackout has been imposed on Gaza. Only Roni Daniel can still join the invading forces and expose their itchy trigger fingers—as he did in his report on Channel 2 on Thursday—and sing their praises. The place so present in the public consciousness, which dictates the security and diplomatic agenda, has been closed by the Israeli authorities to the Israeli media. Long before it was declared a "hostile entity," Gaza had become a closed territory, without any media coverage or documentation. Such is the Israeli freedom of the press.

Anyone who expected such an intolerable reality to stir a protest was proven wrong. In any case, the readers do not want to read about it, the government and the army do not want them to know and the journalists are not yearning to tell. There is no real fight for freedom of media coverage (which is also freedom of expression, information and livelihood)—not by the High Court of Justice, the Press Association and Press Council, or the Association of Civil Rights in Israel. This might have been understandable were it only for a limited time, but how long will this continue? Until all Palestinians join Kadima?

This blocking of media coverage for nearly a year has made us fail seriously in fulfilling our role. The media is not providing the service it is supposed to provide. Even worse, it has surrendered submissively to the prohibitions imposed on it, while blurring the reality. Only a few reporters who still bother to cover Gaza, often entangling their viewers and readers in falsehood, creating the deception that they have just returned from there. Instead of protesting, these journalists collaborate. It is one thing that consumers do not protest about the lack of this service—even *Yes* subscribers remain quiet. But journalists?

It is the state's right and obligation to protect its citizens from unnecessary dangers. But it has no right to prevent those with an essential role to fulfill from doing so. The journalists who crossed at Erez in the past crossed at their own personal and professional responsibility, and signed a statement declaring this. Ron Ben-Yishai, one of the boldest in the field, compared his recent trip to Syria to the work of a technician who climbs up high-tension electricity towers: The work is dangerous, but necessary. And no one thinks of preventing the technician from doing this work. Yet Ben-Yishai, as daring as he may be, can travel to Dir al-Zur in Syria, but not to Dir al-Balah in the Gaza Strip.

With the exception of Burma, not many places in the world are so closed off. It's true that Israel lets foreign journalists enter

Gaza, and this is good, but it is ridiculous when media organizations like *Haaretz*, which still have an interest in covering what's happening, must use foreign sources to tell their readers what's going on there.

But this is not enough. Israelis deserve to read and watch journalism by Israelis. The Italian and Swedish correspondents sent by *Haaretz* to Gaza are professional journalists, but the Israeli reader deserves to receive Israeli media coverage.

It is hard to know what really motivates Israel to close Gaza off in this way. Is it the aspiration, so easy to fulfill, that Gaza will not be exposed here? If, on the other hand, it is an exaggerated concern for our safety, I waive this right. According to our foreign colleagues' reports, it is much safer in Gaza now than it was a year ago, when we still traveled there. Armed gangs no longer roam the streets, and Hamas is even willing to protect Israeli journalists. But how will we know if we're not there?

2008

12

The Lights Have All Been Turned Off

February 4, 2008

One after another, the last lights are being turned off, and a moral gloom is falling upon us as we stand at the edge of an abyss. Just last week, three more lights were turned off. The Winograd Report did not come out clearly against the fact that Israel embarked on a pointless war; the Supreme Court authorized collective punishment and the attorney general concluded that the killing of twelve Israeli citizens and someone from the territories by the police does not warrant a trial. The final keepers of order, the lighthouses of justice and law, are reconciling themselves with the most serious injustices within the institutions of authority, and no one so much as utters a word about it. The upsetting and depressing crop of a single week has drawn the moral portrait of the country.

As expected, the Winograd Committee became irrelevant. It avoided dealing with the first question that should have been on its agenda: Was there any justification for embarking on the war? A committee that says nothing about a country that declares war on its neighbor, kills a thousand of its citizens, causes mass destruction, makes use of horrific munitions and continues to kill dozens of innocents to this day—that is a derelict committee.

If the committee didn't delve into these key issues, then who will? A single, circuitous remark exposed the game: "We do not conclude, and have not concluded, that the decision to embark on war following the abduction [of the two reservists] was not justified." Well, what did they conclude? Despite what the report said, this is what you really hear: It is legitimate in the eyes of the committee to go to war over two abducted soldiers. It is legitimate to utilize the tool of war, to kill indiscriminately, to disproportionately bomb and destroy—all as the preferred first response. No negotiations, no limited military operation, just war—and on such dubious grounds, and of course with such pathetic results. Not a word on the killing and the destruction that we caused in vain. The dignified-looking committee conducted itself like a public information office and supported what many around the world have described as war crimes. A golden opportunity to say something ethical about the language of force that we are always eager to use was missed. The Winograd Committee is a panel lacking a moral backbone, which avoided coming to terms with substantive questions.

On the same day that the committee released its final report, the Supreme Court—that same institution to which all eyes are turned, and over whose influence there is a bitter, ongoing battle—authorized another bug in the works. A panel of justices headed by Court President Dorit Beinisch ruled that Israel is authorized to limit the supply of electricity, gasoline and diesel to the Gaza Strip, "since even these diminished quantities sufficiently meet humanitarian needs."

It is difficult to tell what "humanitarian needs" are according to Beinisch, but in the Gaza Strip 1.5 million people are crying out for fuel, water and electricity. It is fair to ask the court president: Has she ever been exposed to the scenes of wretchedness in the Gaza Strip? Did she ever see the miserable people there carrying fuel in jerrycans from Egypt? Has she considered the cold, which cannot be countered without electricity or fuel? Has she given any serious thought to what happens to children, the infirm and the elderly without these necessities? They are all innocents.

[handwritten annotation: violates article 33 of the Geneva convention]

But the severity of the Supreme Court's decision is not only on the human level: ~~The Supreme Court~~ is authorizing collective punishment, which is specifically forbidden under international law (Article 33 of the Geneva Convention). Henceforth, Israel will no longer be able to complain about attacks against innocents in Israel. If all the residents of the Gaza Strip deserve to be punished because of the Qassam rockets, then maybe all Israelis deserve to be punished because of the occupation.

"This is the difference between Israel, a democracy fighting for its life within the framework of the law, and the terrorist organizations fighting against it," the Supreme Court stated sanctimoniously, like a lowly spokesman from the Foreign Ministry.

"According to the law"? Which law? Not international law. Israel is "fighting for its life"? Well, maybe the Palestinians are fighting a war that is no less justified, against occupation and imprisonment. All this was not on the Supreme Court's agenda.

And last but not least: Attorney General Menachem Mazuz. Twelve citizens and a resident of the territories were killed by the police, and Mazuz ruled that there was no point in initiating a criminal investigation at such a late stage. (The state prosecution decided at the time to delay the investigation until the Or Commission of Inquiry completed its work.) Why shouldn't the court decide? All the excuses, including passing the blame on to the victims' families, who did not permit autopsies, do not in the least diminish the well-founded suspicion: Had the dead been Jewish citizens, this would not have happened; the police would not have killed and the attorney general would not have closed the case.

After all this, people here complain about those who wish to live in a more just country, who are forced to turn to institutions of international law. Who else can they turn to? The Supreme Court? Winograd? The attorney general? Their lights have all been turned off.

13

A Minister of War

March 16, 2008

Defense Minister Ehud Barak is a bitter disappointment. He was the first statesman who dared to suggest brave, though lacking, solutions. Now he has turned into the chief saboteur of any chance for a calm in the fighting, a cease-fire or diplomatic progress. Barak has long forsaken talk of peace. He certainly does not believe in Olmert's peace initiative, and he is trying his best to destroy it.

If you fear Likud Chair Benjamin Netanyahu, how much worse can his potential damage to the peace process be than Barak's? Their rhetoric, as well as their actions, have now become indistinguishable. If calm seems at hand, Barak gives the go-ahead for a silly and dangerous assassination attempt in tranquil Bethlehem—just to rekindle the fire, lest there be a lull.

If there's a lull in Qassams fired, then Barak does everything he can to ensure their renewal, in order to justify the "large-scale op" he intends to make in Gaza. If Palestinian Authority President Mahmoud Abbas is desperately trying to push forward talks, Barak eliminates any chance of bolstering his support. If Hamas suggests a cease-fire, Barak responds: "We will witness harsh scenes in Gaza before a calm is reached." If all's quiet on the northern front, then Israeli pyromania claims Hezbollah's Imad Mughniyah, according to allegations. The security establishment does as it pleases: killing, destroying, barring, seizing funds, issuing orders to close stores and factories in the West

Bank, allowing construction in West Bank settlements, utterly humiliating the Palestinian Authority. It is oblivious to negotiations, Israeli commitments or lofty talk of peace.

Barak, as vociferous as the most zealous settler or Hamas leader, bragged about the Bethlehem operation: "Once again, we've proved that Israel will search and destroy murderers with Jewish blood on their hands." Once again, he has proved that he talks and thinks only of revenge. Is he unaware of the 2006 High Court decision that prohibits targeted killings intended to punish, avenge or deter? Or is he simply ignoring it? A son of one of those killed in Bethlehem said that IDF soldiers promised to put his father—whom he had not seen in a decade—in a body-bag. Something for Barak to take pride in. He has unleashed the Israel Defense Forces on the Palestinians and ordered shows of force, including the failed Gaza op, which killed 120 people and produced zero results. Hamas had been talking about a cease-fire, and who rejected it? Israel, the peace objector.

Instead of issuing a clear IDF order to calm the area to coincide with the government's new initiative, Barak is doing everything he can to disrupt it. And we have yet to mention morality: Long gone are the days when targeted killings were disputed, when people argued that they were carried out only against "ticking bombs." Now even retired terrorists are being killed in cold blood in their cars. They are charged with old crimes and executed without trial, instead of being arrested, a method that would prevent the next outbreak of violence while also remaining moral.

Barak is not alone. Though his political party is small and ailing, it is nonetheless a political party, and its silence is abominable. Shas can milk more and more construction plans for the settlements, but Labor is not even trying to achieve its goals. Where have Amir Peretz, Ami Ayalon, Yuli Tamir, Shelly Yachimovich, Colette Avital, Ghaleb Majadele and Ophir Pines-Paz gone at a time that their party leader is leading them to oblivion? Why do they not raise their voices in protest? And why doesn't the prime minister restrain his defense minister?

When the conflagration begins—very soon, because of Barak's policies—none of them will be free from blame. They will all be remembered as full participants in the terrible disgrace. Then we'll recall how there used to be hope, but that the Labor leader, of all people, did everything he could to sabotage it. And no one did a thing.

14

With Friends Like These

March 23, 2008

The amount of support being shown for Israel these days is almost embarrassing. The parade of highly placed foreign guests and the warm reception received by Israeli statesmen abroad have not been seen for quite some time. Who hasn't come to visit lately? We've had everyone from the German chancellor to the leading frontrunner for the American presidency, and the secretary-general of the United Nations is on his way. A visit to Israel has become de rigueur for foreign pols. If you haven't been here, you're nowhere.

The visitors are taken, of course, to the Yad Vashem Holocaust memorial, the Western Wall and now to Sderot as well—the new national pilgrimage site. A few also pay a perfunctory visit to Ramallah; no one goes to the Gaza Strip, and they all have nothing but praise for Israel. Not a word of criticism—about the occupation, about Israel's violent operations in the territories, about the siege and the starving—with the exception of a few vague remarks on the need for a solution. Israel squeezes the Sderot "informational" lemon for all it's worth. The mix of Sderot and the Holocaust, international islamophobia and Hamas rule in Gaza do the trick. Israel hasn't scored this kind of foreign-policy success since the days of the Oslo Accords. To judge by the declarations of our foreign guests and our hosts abroad, no other state in the world is more loved than we. A state that imposes a siege that is almost unprecedented in the world today in terms of its cruelty, and adopts an official policy of assassination, is embraced by the family of nations, if we are to judge by the words of the many statesmen who cross our doorstep.

It is, of course, pleasant to revel in this wave of support, but it is an illusion. Public opinion, in most of the countries whose leaders are heaping all that praise upon us, is not joining in. Israel remains a state without approval, sometimes even outcast and despised. The world sees images from Gaza on television— in comparison, Sderot looks like a resort—and it draws its own conclusions. The natural sense of justice that dictates support for the freedom struggles of oppressed people such as the Tibetans dictates natural support for the Palestinian struggle for liberation. The fact that it is a struggle between a Palestinian David and an Israeli Goliath only adds to the story. With the exception of the United States, the world is indeed against us, apart from its statesmen. Therefore, we must not give in to the illusion: The current bout of official support for us is not genuine.

Also not genuine is the idea that blind, unconditional friendship is actually friendship. The support for Israel as a just enterprise that is extended by most of the West does not mean accepting all of its caprices. A true friend of Israel, one that is sincerely concerned for its fate, is only that friend who dares to express sharp criticism of Israel's policy of occupation, which poses the most serious risk to its future, and who also takes practical steps to end it. Most of the "friendly" statesmen do not understand this.

The stance of the European leaders is particularly perplexing. We're not speaking about the United States, with its Jewish and Christian lobbies, but rather opinionated Europe; it, too, has lost its ability to act as an honest broker, the type that wields its influence to bring an end to the conflict that endangers it, too. We need Europe, the peace needs Europe, but official Europe covers its eyes and automatically falls in line with the United

States, its blind support for Israel and its boycott of Gaza. Angela Merkel, who received such a royal reception here last week, did not bring up any controversial issue in her speech at the Knesset. And so, her "historic" speech turned into a hollow one.

The same behavior was displayed by her colleague in the European leadership, French President Nicolas Sarkozy, during the visit to his country of President Shimon Peres. The Israeli flags waving along the Champs-Élysées and the much-talked-about Israeli booth at the Paris Book Fair could not hide the fact that many French citizens are pained by the occupation. By not speaking about the siege on Gaza, the starvation imposed on it and the killing of hundreds of its people, Europe's leaders are not meeting their political and moral obligations. Those who believe that only honest international intervention can bring an end to the occupation find themselves desperate and disappointed. Europe, precisely that continent that carries justifiable feelings of guilt about the Jewish Holocaust, should have found another way to come to Israel's aid. Saccharine visits and sweet speeches in fact express a deep disrespect for Israel—and for European public opinion.

This blind friendship enables Israel to do whatever it wants. The days have passed in which every mobile home erected in the territories and every targeted assassination were carefully considered out of fear of international criticism. Israel now has carte blanche to kill, destroy and settle. The United States long ago gave up the role of honest broker, and Europe is now following in its footsteps. How depressing: With friends like these, Israel almost doesn't need enemies.

Europe should have done more should felt more responsible

Carte blanche

15

A Conditional EU Upgrade

June 15, 2008

How pleasant it is to be an official representative of Israel in Europe right now. It hasn't been this pleasant for a long time. And not just because of the spectacular spring in the Luxembourg Gardens in Paris, the crowded pubs in Athens or the young people sunbathing nude in Stockholm. This is about the fresh sympathy for Israel blowing in from almost every capital. French newspapers went all out for our sixtieth anniversary, Israeli women soldiers were featured on the covers of magazines, and even the Swedish papers lost a little of their interest in the Palestinians' suffering, which had for years won such deep sympathy.

Last week, when the Olof Palme International Center in Stockholm held a symposium on peace in the Middle East, a scandal broke out because the organizers dared to invite Azam Tamimi, a professor of Islamic studies and Hamas sympathizer from London. Even in Sweden. This sympathy for Israel, along with seething antipathy for Palestinians, Arabs and Muslims, includes, of course, active European participation in the boycott of Gaza and Hamas, which may reach new heights this week. The Council of Foreign Ministers of the European Union is slated tomorrow to discuss upgrading Israel's standing in the EU, and later in the week ministers of the EU member states will also do so. It only takes opposition by one country to prevent the upgrade of ties, which would have significant economic ramifications for Israel.

But there is a good chance that exactly as Europe decided unanimously to boycott Gaza, it will unanimously say yes to an upgrade of Israel's ties with the EU. For official Israel, this is excellent news. Perhaps for the first time, a very strange set of circumstances prevails: Europe, which holds high the standard of human rights and liberty, is boycotting the occupied entity, and as if that weren't enough, it is even upgrading its ties with the occupier. While Europe is perceived by most Israelis as hostile to Israel, not to say anti-Semitic, its governments are uniting to support Israel almost no matter what it does.

Europe's blind obedience to the United States, which led it into Afghanistan and Iraq, combined with guilt over the Holocaust, is manifest in its relationship toward us. Xenophobia, and particularly hatred of Muslims, Hamas's rise in Gaza, and that organization's perception in Europe as part of a dangerous Islamic conspiracy whose other members are Al-Qaeda and Hezbollah, are now also finding expression in the relationship to Israel.

It is true that Israel's representatives continue to complain bitterly about hostility. Israel's envoy to London last week lamented that Britain had become a hotbed of radical anti-Israel views; it always pays to complain. It is also true that public opinion in Europe is still more sympathetic to the Palestinians. But the European governments are turning their backs on this sentiment and are promoting a quite amazingly sympathetic policy toward Israel. There is practically no country that has not sent an official to Israel recently; they are all rushing to Sderot to take their picture with a Qassam, and they are staying away from Gaza in droves, despite the much greater suffering there. This false magic charm should not be allowed to trick us. This is not good news for those who wish for an end to the Israeli occupation and still believe that Europe can and should play a useful role in achieving peace in the region. Europe, which is now incomprehensibly and blindly following the United States, is not just ignoring the values it proclaims; it is also going to lose any possibility to influence the region. That is not good for the Middle East, and it is bad for Europe, too, in whose backyard our conflict begins.

We already have a one-sided mediator of the type that gives Israel free rein to follow every whim of its occupation: America. We have no need for another. Europe's special status—as Israel's major economic market that maintains an extensive network of relations with the Arab world as well—is eroding. Instead, we are getting a West that no longer makes demands on Israel, comes to terms with the criminal occupation and is heavy-handed only when it comes to the Palestinians. True, Europe is also the biggest donor to the Palestinian Authority, but in so doing it subsidizes the occupation, nothing more.

When PA Prime Minister Salam Fayyad, the darling of Israel and the United States, dared recently to work against the upgrade, Israel quickly hit the PA in its pocketbook and confiscated the tax money belonging to it—a scandal in itself. This same thing will be done to whoever tries to demand that Europe maintain some measure of balance.

Europe must come to its senses now. It must condition the upgrade of relations with Israel on a series of practical steps Israel must take, in the spirit of its declared values. Want an upgrade? Please conduct yourselves according to international law, please respect the most basic human rights, please lift the siege on Gaza. That is how the EU behaves toward the rest of the countries knocking at its door. An unconditional upgrade will be a prize for settlements, a medal for siege, closures and starvation. Is that the way Europe wants to see itself? Lavishing gifts on the occupier, boycotting the occupied and becoming an American puppet?

16

Caterpillar Fashion

July 24, 2008

Israel might be able to go on claiming that it will not be the first to introduce nuclear weapons into the Middle East, but it cannot do the same regarding another weapon of mass destruction: the bulldozer. The claim that terror has adopted an original new weapon, a "new fashion" as the public security minister put it, once again shows how convenient it is for us to present a one-sided and distorted picture.

The bulldozer as a destructive and even lethal weapon was not invented by the Palestinians. They are merely imitating an Israeli "fashion" that is as old as the state, or at least as old as the occupation. Let us forget for a moment the 416 villages Israel wiped off the face of the earth in 1948—that was before there were D9 bulldozers—and focus on a more modern trend. In Israel's hands, the bulldozer has become one of the most terrifying weapons in the territories. The only difference between the Palestinians' murderous bulldozer and the Israeli one is in color and size. As usual, ours is much, much bigger. There is no similarity between the small backhoe the Palestinian terrorist was driving and the fearsome D9 driven by Israel Defense Forces soldiers.

From the dawn of the occupation, Caterpillar has been a major arms supplier to Israel, no less than those who provide planes, cannons and tanks. Not for nothing are peace activists trying to call for a boycott of the company: Israel has sown almost unimaginable destruction using heavy equipment. Go to Rafah, stopping in Khan Yunis on the way, and see the results of the destruction scattered there to this day. Whole neighborhoods razed, the contents of houses—possessions and memories—crushed under the treads. Have you ever seen a street that has been "stripped" by a bulldozer? Cars are crushed like tin cans and homes become piles of rubble, along with their contents. Any street in Rafah looks much worse than King David Street in Jerusalem this week.

In 2004, for example, 10,704 Palestinians were made homeless after the IDF destroyed 1,404 homes, mostly in Gaza, due to "operational needs." In the Jenin refugee camp, Israel destroyed 560 homes; the legendary bulldozer driver "Kurdi" told how he would swig whiskey as he "turned Jenin into a soccer field." In Operation Rainbow, another bulldozer operation, Israel destroyed 120 homes in one day in the Brazil camp in Rafah. Only someone who was in Rafah and Khan Yunis at the time can understand what our excellent bulldozers did.

Do not say that our bulldozers only destroy but do not kill. What killed peace activist Rachel Corrie if not a bulldozer—whose driver, according to witnesses, saw her before he crushed her to death? And what about the Shubi family in the Nablus casbah—a grandfather, two aunts, a mother and two children—crushed under bulldozers? And who killed Jamal Faid, a handicapped man from the Jenin camp, whose wheelchair was found under the ruins of his house, with his body never recovered? Was that not bulldozer terror?

The Palestinians discovered the bulldozer quite late. What is good for us is good for them. And how do our security experts propose to fight the new fashion? By demolishing the houses of the terrorists—with bulldozers, of course.

17

Neither Officer
Nor Gentleman

July 31, 2008

Brigadier General Moshe "Chico" Tamir is a devoted and loving father who decided to let his fourteen-year-old son drive a military all-terrain vehicle. Being the law-abiding organization that it is, the Israel Defense Forces probed the incident, calling it "serious." As a result, Tamir's promotion may be put on hold and he may be indicted. Certainly, a brigade commander who tried to cover up his son's accident by lying deserves to be punished. But the commander of the Gaza Brigade deserves much worse for acts considerably more serious—acts that the world defines as war crimes and for which no one has been held accountable.

I would like Tamir, the dedicated father, to meet a girl the same age as his beloved son, a girl whose world fell apart when she was fourteen years old. I saw Islam Athamneh in mourning in November 2006, in the courtyard of her destroyed house in Beit Hanoun. She lost eight family members: her mother, grandmother, grandfather, aunts, uncles and cousins. They fled their house when it was struck by a shell and were killed by another onslaught. The legs of her three-year-old brother Abdullah were blown off. Islam, whose father had died years earlier, became an orphan.

The soldiers who fired the eleven shells at houses in Beit Hanoun were under the command of Tamir, the dedicated father who let his son take a Tomcar for a joyride. Some twenty-two people were killed in the shelling and another forty were hurt. Most lost limbs or sustained head wounds.

It was the Gaza Brigade commander, Tamir, who was responsible for that atrocity, but the IDF quickly absolved him of blame. Instead, they placed it on a faulty electronic component in the gun barrel. It was the chip, not Chico, that was to blame. In the seven days before the heinous shelling, which violates international law, Tamir's troops managed to kill eighty Palestinians, forty of whom were innocent civilians, as part of Operation Autumn Clouds. Their blood was shed, but apparently their deaths pale in significance to the Tomcar affair as far as the army is concerned. After all, what's a bit of unlawful killing en masse next to illegally driving an ATV?

backward priorities

If indicted, it won't be the first time Tamir has been tried in court. In the summer of 2002, when he was the commander of the Golani Brigade, his soldiers fired a tank shell at a grocers' market in Jenin. That, too, was a war crime, but not to Israel. A fifty-three-year-old vendor and three children—two of whom were brothers—died in the shelling. These children had fathers who loved their sons just as much as Tamir loves his. The Military Advocate General believed Tamir was guilty of negligence, but a court cleared him of all charges. A few weeks later, Tamir's tanks fired another shell at the same market. This time they killed a vendor who was loading onions into his Peugeot 504.

Former IDF chief Moshe Ya'alon once said about this officer and gentleman that he needs "reeducating" because of endemic disciplinary problems in his brigade. The person who bragged that his brigade behaved like Rottweilers, who thought more violence should be used against Palestinians, who said that the destruction his soldiers wreaked in a Jenin refugee camp did not "cause him any moral dilemmas"—this man may now finally be punished. And for what? A Tomcar. And what might just spare him? For all his misdoings, he may be cleared of blame because he is considered a "well-respected and important" officer in the IDF.

18

"The Ebb, the Tide, the Sighs"

November 13, 2008

Mohammed Masalah is now in hospital, feeble and pale, one leg in a cast held in place by iron screws. The young fisherman is in constant pain. His mother does not leave his bedside. A blind Palestinian physician takes him for a brief physiotherapy session in the corridor. Masalah leans on a walker. The blind orthopedist encourages him to take one step and then another, but the pain defeats him and he asks to be taken back to bed.

The sea is the same sea and the Arabs are the same Arabs, as an Israeli prime minister once said. Only the cease-fire is no longer the same cease-fire. On land and in the air it is generally maintained, but not at sea. There, Israeli forces continue to shoot at fishermen from besieged Gaza, people who are trying to wrest from the sea a living that is so difficult to make on land.

Gaza's 40,000 fishermen have been deprived of their livelihood. Before the siege, they caught 3,000 tons of fish a year; now it is 500 tons. The fishing season begins with the advent of winter, when schools of fish migrate from the Nile Delta and the waters off Turkey toward the Gaza area. But few of them are now ensnared in the nets of Gaza's fishermen. Today, most of the fish can be found about ten miles offshore, in an area that is off-limits to the fishermen. Israel has restricted them to a six-mile limit, though sometimes navy boats attack at three miles—just to keep the fishermen honest.

50 million liters of sewage?! [handwritten annotation]

The siege makes it hard to obtain fuel for the fishing vessels, and the sea is polluted with 50 million liters of sewage every day, following the collapse of the sewage infrastructure in the Gaza Strip. Israel's fish markets are also closed to merchants from Gaza.

Hardest of all, though, are the naval attacks. Every few days the International Solidarity Movement (ISM) publishes reports from its volunteers in Gaza about attacks on fishermen. Sometimes the naval boats ram the wretched craft, sometimes the sailors use high-pressure water hoses on the fishermen, hurtling them into the sea, and sometimes they open lethal fire on them. The boat of Masalah and his friend Ahmad Bardaawi came under such fire for about twenty minutes, until the two managed to get away, with Bardaawi rowing for all he was worth. A bullet slammed into Masalah's leg, however, and it was hours before he reached the hospital, after a long, exhausting and bloody journey along the Rafah coast with his friend. The physicians in the Khan Yunis hospital wanted to amputate. Now, with Israel's permission, Masalah is being treated in a hospital in East Jerusalem, and his leg will probably be saved.

"The ebb, the tide, the sighs / The sailor who whitens the trunks of tamarisks / The gatherers of conches collect on the shore / Seagulls' broken keening for desperate love," Meir Banai sings, in the words of Natan Yonatan's poem "The Fisherman's Prayer." There is nothing very romantic about Masalah's story. Certainly there is no keening of seagulls, and what is desperate is the need to provide for his family, and the prayer that he will one day be able to walk on both legs again.

A fisherman will get up at around 2 a.m. and walk about three kilometers in the dark to the shoreline, where a rowboat awaits him. There's no money for fuel, and in any case it's hard to find fuel in Gaza, so it's row, row, row your boat—as far out as Israel allows. Dabur-class patrol boats lurk everywhere. As everyone knows, the occupation of Gaza has ended, and the Strip has been completely liberated.

Masalah is a nineteen-year-old twelfth-grader, the son of a fisherman from the Tel al-Sultan neighborhood of Rafah. His father no longer goes out to sea. Since the age of sixteen, Masalah has been getting his schooling in the morning and fishing at night. He has about 700 fishhooks that he throws into the water, hoping for the best. Now is the season for groupers and red snapper, known in Gaza as *farfur*. On a very good night he catches fifteen kilograms of fish, two kilos on a bad night, and there are nights when he catches nothing. Fish go for NIS 50 per kilo in an abundant season; double that when there are no fish. Masalah splits the earnings with Bardaawi. Their GPS tells them where to stop: 1,800 meters from the shore, no more. At first light, they head home to do their homework and study for exams.

"If the Jews have a good 'shift,' they let us stay; if not, they start shooting and we have to escape," Masalah says in a weak voice from his hospital bed. About a month and a half ago, Israeli sailors broke his oars.

The night of October 5th was no different than usual. Masalah's mother woke him, and at 2 a.m. he met up with Bardaawi and they headed out to sea. At 3:30 the two young fishermen reached the limit allowed them and cast anchor. Close by was the rowboat belonging to Bardaawi's cousin. They were about to cast their hooks when they noticed a flashing red light: The Dabur was lying in wait, with all lights except the red one turned off.

The firing began instantly, on both sides of the boat and over their heads. Masalah says that this time no warning flares were fired, as is usually done. No one bellowed at them through a megaphone, warning them to move away. Indeed, the soldiers always yell at them to get out of the way, but not that night. The young men were about seventy meters from the patrol boat, and Masalah was hit in the first volley. His leg felt as though it had caught fire, and he started to shake all over. Bardaawi grabbed the oars and started to row frantically, the Dabur speeding along in their wake. Masalah, shouting with excruciating pain, pressed on his leg to try to stanch the bleeding. The shooting lasted about twenty minutes, he says.

Reaching safe haven at last, they sent one of the children on the beach to find help. The ambulance was slow to arrive, so a vehicle belonging to the Palestinian Coast Guard rushed Masalah to Yusuf Al-Najjar Hospital in Rafah. There was no physician on duty. While they were waiting there, the ambulance showed up, and it took Masalah to the European Hospital in Khan Yunis. (He was not taken to Shifa Hospital in Gaza City, because the physicians there are on strike against Hamas.)

Masalah's bleeding worsened, chills ran through his body and he lost consciousness. The doctor said the leg would have to be amputated, but Masalah's family begged him to wait. They wanted to transfer him to a hospital in Israel, but the Palestinian Authority refused to pay for that, and suggested Makassed Hospital in East Jerusalem. It took three full weeks to collect all the permits necessary to leave Gaza, but finally Masalah and his mother were granted "hospitalization authorization" from the Interior Ministry of the State of Israel, signed by Major Azhar Ghanem, head of civil coordination. The permit was valid for one day, October 26, 2008, from 5 a.m. until 7 p.m. By the time they got through the Erez checkpoint and reached the hospital, it was already 4 o'clock.

Masalah and his mother, for whom this was their first trip outside the Gaza Strip, are now "illegally present" in East Jerusalem. She spends the nights in an armchair by his bed, and he is focusing on trying to rehabilitate his leg. He has had one operation and will need two more.

The IDF Spokesman's Unit has stated in response that "an investigation with the Israel Navy found that no casualties were identified in this event. On the night between October 4 and October 5, two Palestinian fishing boats went past the area in which fishing is permitted. The navy launched warning flares and implemented deterrent fire only, with the emphasis on avoiding casualties. An additional check with the navy, at the correspondent's request, did not turn up any new findings."

19

Obama Should Not
Be Israel's Friend

November 9, 2008

The march of parochialism started right away. The tears of excitement invoked by US President-elect Barack Obama's wonderful speech had not yet dried, and back here people were already delving into the only real question they could think to ask: Is this good or bad for Israel? One after another, the analysts and politicians got up—all of them representing one single school of thought, of course—and began prophesizing.

They spoke with the caution that the situation required, gritting their teeth as though their mouths were full of pebbles, trying to soothe all the fears and concerns. They searched and found signs in Obama: the promising appointment of the Israeli ex-patriots' son, whose father belonged to the Irgun, and maybe also Dennis Ross and Dan Kurtzer and Martin Indyk, who may, God willing, be included in the new administration.

But in the background, a dark cloud hovered above. Careful: danger. This man, who had associated with Palestinian ex-pats, who speaks of human rights, who favors diplomacy over war, who wants to engage Iran in dialogue, who will allocate more funding for America's social needs than to weapons exports—he may not be the sort of "friend of Israel" that we have come to love in Washington, the kind of friend we have grown accustomed to.

What's the panic all about? The truth needs to be said: At the base of all of these anxieties is the fear that this president will push Israel to end the occupation and move toward peace.

May Obama *not* be a "friend of Israel." May the great change he is promising not omit his country's Mideast policy. May Obama herald not only a new America, but also a new Middle East.

When we say that someone is a "friend of Israel," we mean a friend of the occupation, a believer in Israel's self-armament, a champion of its language of strength and a supporter of all its regional delusions. When we say someone is a "friend of Israel," we mean someone who will give Israel carte blanche for any violent adventure it desires, for rejecting peace and for building in the territories.

Israel's greatest friend in the White House, outgoing US President George W. Bush, was someone like that. There is no other country where this man, who brought a string of disasters down upon his own nation and the world, would receive any degree of prestige and respect. Only in Israel.

Only in Israel does the prime minister place George Bush's portrait in the den of his private home. Only in Israel does the prime minister travel to visit him in the White House.

That's because Bush was a "friend of Israel." Israel's greatest friend, in fact. Bush let Israel embark on an unnecessary war in Lebanon. He did not prevent the construction of a single outpost. He may have encouraged Israel, in secret, to bomb Iran. He did not pressure Israel to move ahead with peace talks; he even held up negotiations with Syria. He did not reproach Israel for its policy of targeted killings.

Bush also supported the siege on Gaza and participated in the boycott of Hamas, which gained power in a democratic election initiated by his own administration.

That's just how we like US presidents. They give us a green light to do as we please. They fund, equip and arm us, and then they sit tight. Such is the classic friend of Israel—a friend who is an enemy, an enemy of peace and an enemy to Israel.

Let us hope that Obama will not be like them. That he will reveal himself to be a *true* friend of Israel. That he will put his whole weight behind a deep American involvement in the Middle East. That he will try to solve the Iranian issue through negotiation—the only effective means. That he will help end the siege on Gaza and the boycott of Hamas, that he will push Israel and Syria to make peace, that he will spur Israel and the Palestinians to reach a settlement.

We should hope that Obama will help Israel help itself, because that is how real friendship is measured. That he will criticize Israel's policies when he must, because that, too, is a test of true friendship.

Let him use his clout to end the occupation and dismantle the settlement project. Let him remember that human and civil rights also apply to the Palestinians, not only to black Americans. And apropos world peace, he needs to start with peace in the Middle East, home to the most dangerous of conflicts, which has been threatening the world for a century now, and is feeding international terrorism.

A true friend of Israel needs to remember that Israel may be "the only democracy in the Middle East," but not in its own backyard. That next to Sderot, which Obama has visited, is Gaza. That "common values" must not include a cruel occupation. That friendship does not mean blind and automatic support.

Let Obama speak with Iran, Hezbollah and Hamas, as often as he can and with whomever is willing to talk. And let him do it before the next war, not after it. Let him remember that he has the power to do all that.

Changing the Middle East was within the reach of each and every US president who could have pressured Israel and put an end to the occupation. Most of them kept their hands off as if it were a hot potato, all in the name of a wonderful friendship.

So bring us an American president who is not another dreadful "friend of Israel," an Obama who won't blindly follow the positions of the Jewish lobby and the Israeli government.

You did promise change, didn't you?

20

Talk with Hamas

December 21, 2008

The situation in the south is depressing. Qassam rockets are being fired out of a territory beset by boycott, siege and intolerable conditions at Israeli communities whose situation is no more tolerable, and the Israeli defense establishment admits it has no real response. With the exception of a few loud-mouthed politicians, including Kadima head Tzipi Livni (who have elections in mind), most level-headed politicians know the truth: There is no military solution. No wide-reaching or small operation; no targeted killing or bombing will help. Nor is there a military solution for the situation of abducted soldier Gilad Shalit.

So what's left to do but shrug? Gaza is banished and impoverished, Sderot is threatened and despairs, and no one dares try to break the vicious cycle.

Even outgoing Prime Minister Ehud Olmert, who in the twilight of his political career has excelled at making blunt and courageous remarks, has done nothing. If any debate is held over what course of action to pursue, it is either for or against a "wide-scale operation." Meanwhile, analysts sit in news studios and dispatch advice, all of it belligerent and militaristic. Politicians, generals and the public all know that any substantial incursion into the Gaza Strip will be a catastrophe. Still no one dares ask why, for heaven's sake, don't we try to talk directly with Hamas?

Gaza has an established authority, which seized power democratically and then forcibly, and has proven that it has the
power to control the territory. That, in itself, isn't bad news
after a period of anarchy. But Israel and the world don't like
Hamas. They want to overthrow it, but their diabolical scheme
isn't working out. The two-year siege and boycott—which
has included starvation, blackouts and bombardments—have
produced no sign that Hamas is weaker. On the contrary: The
cease-fire was violated first by Israel with its unnecessary operation of blowing up a tunnel.

The theory everybody already knew to be false—that the
political choice of a people could be changed through violence,
that the Gazans could be made into Zionists by being abused—
was put into practice anyway. Now we finally have to change
course, to do what nobody has tried before, if only because we
have no other choice.

Any argument against such an attempt does not hold water.
Hamas doesn't recognize Israel—what does it matter? Hamas
is a fundamentalist movement—that's irrelevant. Hamas will
decline holding talks—let's challenge it. Direct talks with
Hamas will weaken Palestinian Authority President Mahmoud
Abbas—he's weak anyway.

What does Israel have to lose, besides the much-anticipated
large-scale operation, which it can carry out any time? Why not
try the diplomatic option before the military one, and not the
other way around like we're used to?

Events seem even more bizarre because Olmert, the belated
man of peace, realizes he has nothing to lose and is currently
advancing talks with Syria. His trip to Turkey tomorrow over
negotiations with Damascus is praiseworthy, but on his way to
Ankara he should visit the Erez crossing with Gaza and call on
Hamas leader Ismail Haniyeh to meet him for talks over the
security situation and the Shalit prisoner exchange. That would
change everything. Israel has nothing to lose. Our policy is such

that we don't talk to Abbas because he's too weak, and we don't talk to Haniyeh because he's too strong.

Israel is negotiating with Hamas through Egyptian channels anyway. Isn't it more reasonable to try holding direct talks? Let's not forget the tired cliché: Negotiations are held between the bitterest of enemies. So it goes and so it will be even after more blood is spilled, so why not try to avoid such bloodshed? We've already been in this predicament. For years we said no to talks with the Palestinian Liberation Organization. What did that yield? Nothing but an unnecessary and cursed intifada, after which we finally started negotiating.

There's no chance that Hamas will change its stripes entirely, but direct talks may be more pragmatic than they seem. Hamas has some reasonable leaders who value life and want to improve the wretched situation of their nation. They, too, realize the current situation is a dead end for both us and them.

Israel should offer to lift the siege and boycott in return for a long-term calm. But we're preoccupied with ourselves: When do we start bombing? When do we start conquering? Who's our next target for elimination? That all this has already been tried and proven to lead nowhere has not budged us from our stubborn position.

That's why I address the prime minister in a desperate final call: Break the taboo. Bravely urge your counterpart Haniyeh to meet with you. As you said over the weekend about talks with Syria: "How can we be sure if we don't try?" Likud's Benjamin Netanyahu, Labor's Ehud Barak or Livni might not like it, but that certainly shouldn't concern you anymore.

21

The Neighborhood Bully Strikes Again

December 29, 2008

Israel embarked yesterday on yet another unnecessary, ill-fated war. On July 16, 2006, four days after the start of the Second Lebanon War, I wrote: "Every neighborhood has one, a loud-mouthed bully who shouldn't be provoked into anger . . . Not that the bully's not right—someone did harm him. But the reaction, what a reaction!"

Two and a half years later, these words repeat themselves, to our horror, with chilling precision. Within the span of a few hours on a Saturday afternoon, the IDF sowed death and destruction on a scale that the Qassam rockets never approached in all their years, and Operation "Cast Lead" is only in its infancy.

Once again, Israel's violent responses, even if there is justification for them, exceed all proportion and cross every red line of humaneness, morality, international law and wisdom.

What began yesterday in Gaza is a war crime and betrays the foolishness of a country. History's bitter irony: A government that went into a futile war two months after its establishment—today nearly everyone acknowledges as much—embarks on another doomed war two months before the end of its term.

In the interim, the loftiness of peace was on the tip of the tongue of Ehud Olmert, a man who uttered some of the most courageous words ever spoken by a prime minister. Yes, the

over reaction

loftiness of peace on the tip of his tongue—and two fruitless
wars in his sheath. Joining him is his defense minister, Ehud
Barak, the leader of the so-called left-wing party, who plays the
role of senior accomplice to the crime.

Israel did not exhaust the diplomatic processes before embarking yesterday on another dreadful campaign of killing and ruin.
The Qassams that rained down on the communities near Gaza
were intolerable, even though they did not sow death. But the
response to them needs to be fundamentally different: diplomatic efforts to restore the cease-fire—the same one that was
initially breached, one should remember, by Israel when it
unnecessarily bombed a tunnel—and then, if those efforts fail, a
measured, gradual military response. *measured response*

But no. It's all or nothing. The IDF launched a war yesterday, *after*
the goal of which is, as usual, to confirm our fond hope that *all*
someone is watching over us. Blood will now flow like water. *else*
Besieged and impoverished Gaza, the city of refugees, will pay *exhaust*
the main price. But blood will also be unnecessarily spilled on
our side. In its foolishness, Hamas brought this on itself and on
its people, but this does not excuse Israel's overreaction.

The history of the Middle East is repeating itself with devastating precision. Only the frequency is increasing. If we enjoyed
nine years of quiet between the Yom Kippur War and the First
Lebanon War, now we launch wars every two years. As such,
Israel proves that there is no connection between its public-
relations talking-points about peace, and its belligerent conduct.

Israel also proves that it has not internalized the lessons of the
previous war. Once again, this war was preceded by a frighteningly uniform public dialogue in which only one voice was
heard—that which called for striking, destroying, starving and
killing; that which incited and prodded for the commission of
war crimes.

Once again the commentators sat in television studios yesterday and hailed the combat jets that bombed police stations,

where officers responsible for maintaining order on the streets work. Once again, they urged against letting up and in favor of continuing the assault. Once again, the journalists described the pictures of the damaged house in Netivot as "a difficult scene." Once again, we had the nerve to complain about how the world was transmitting images from Gaza. And once again we need to wait a few more days until an alternative voice finally rises from the darkness, a voice of wisdom and morality.

In another week or two, those same pundits who called for blows and more blows will compete among themselves in leveling criticism at this war. And once again this will be gravely late.

The pictures that flooded television screens around the world yesterday showed a parade of corpses and wounded being loaded into and unloaded from the trunks of the private cars that transported them to the only hospital in Gaza worthy of being called a hospital. Perhaps we once again need to remember that we are dealing with a wretched, battered strip of land, most of whose population consists of the children of refugees who have endured inhuman tribulations.

For two and a half years they have been caged and ostracized by the whole world. The line of thinking that states that through war we will gain new allies in the Strip, that abusing the population and killing its sons will sear this into their consciousness, and that a military operation would suffice to topple an entrenched regime and thus replace it with another one friendlier to us is no more than lunacy.

Hezbollah was not weakened as a result of the Second Lebanon War; to the contrary, it was strengthened. Hamas will not be weakened due to the Gaza war; to the contrary, it, too, will grow stronger. In a short time, after the parade of corpses and wounded ends, we will arrive at a fresh cease-fire, as occurred after Lebanon, exactly like the one that could have been forged without this superfluous war.

In the meantime, let us now let the IDF win, as they say. A hero against the weak, it bombed dozens of targets from the air yesterday, and the pictures of blood and fire are designed to show Israelis, Arabs and the entire world that the neighborhood bully's strength has yet to wane. When the bully is on a rampage, nobody can stop him.

22

Making Monsters of Our Finest Young Men

December 31, 2008

Our finest young men are attacking Gaza now. Good boys from good homes are doing bad things. Most of them are eloquent, impressive, self-confident, often even highly principled in their own eyes, and on Black Saturday dozens of them set out to bomb some of the targets in our "target bank" for the Gaza Strip.

They set out to bomb the graduation ceremony for young police officers who had found that rare Gaza commodity, a job, and massacred them by the dozen. They bombed a mosque, killing five sisters of the Balousha family, the youngest of whom was only four. They bombed a police station, hitting a doctor nearby; she lies in a vegetative state in Shifa Hospital, which is full to bursting with wounded and dead. They bombed a university that we in Israel call the Palestinian Rafael, the equivalent of Israel's weapons developer, and destroyed student dormitories. They dropped hundreds of bombs out of clear blue skies free of all resistance.

In four days they killed 375 people. They did not, and could not, distinguish between a Hamas official and his children, between a traffic cop and a Qassam launch operator, between a weapons cache and a health clinic, between the first and second floors of a densely populated apartment building with dozens of

[handwritten: Killed indiscr; couldn't tell it was humans]

children inside. According to reports, about half of the people killed were innocent civilians. We're not complaining about the pilots' accuracy; it cannot be otherwise when the weapon is a plane and the objective is a tiny, crowded strip of land. But our excellent pilots are effectively bullies now. As in training flights, they bomb undisturbed, facing neither an air force nor a defense system.

It is hard to judge what they are thinking, how they feel. It's unlikely to be relevant, anyway. They are measured by their actions. In any event, from an altitude of thousands of feet, the picture looks as sterile as a Rorschach inkblot. Lock on to the target, press the button and then a black column of smoke. Another "successful hit." None see the effects of their actions on the ground. Their heads must surely be filled with Gaza horror stories—they themselves have never been there—as if there aren't a million and a half people residing there who only want to live with a minimum of honor, some of them young like the pilots themselves, with dreams of studying, working, raising a family, but who will have no chance to fulfill their dreams, with or without the bombing.

Do the pilots think about the children of refugees whose parents and grandparents have already been driven from their lives? Do they think about the thousands of people they have left permanently disabled in a place without a single hospital worthy of the name, and no rehabilitation centers at all? Do they think about the burning hatred they are planting, not only in Gaza but in other corners of the world where people are watching the horrific images on television?

It was not the pilots who decided to go to war, but they are the subcontractors. The real accounting must, of course, be with the decision makers, but the pilots are their partners. When they return home they will be welcomed with all the respect and honor we reserve for them. It appears that not only will no one try to provoke moral questioning among them, but that

[handwritten: pilots = subcontractors of the war]

they are considered the real heroes of this cursed war. The Israel
Defense Forces spokesman is already going over the top with
praise in his daily briefings for the "wonderful work" they are
doing. He too, of course, completely ignores the images from
Gaza. After all, these are not sadistic Border Police officers beating up Arabs in the alleys of Nablus and the center of Hebron,
or cruel undercover soldiers who shoot their targets point-blank
in cold blood. These, as we have said, are our finest young men.
Maybe if they were to confront the results of their "wonderful work" even once, they would regret their decisions, and
they would reconsider the effects of their actions. If they were
to go just once to Jerusalem's Alyn Hospital Pediatric and
Adolescent Rehabilitation Center, where for nearly three years
Marya Aman, now seven, has been hospitalized—she is a quadri-
plegic who runs her wheelchair, and her life, with her chin—
they would be shocked. This adorable little girl was hit by a
missile in Gaza that killed almost her entire family, which was
the handiwork of our pilots.

But all of this is well hidden from the pilots' eyes. They are
only doing their job, as the saying goes; only following orders
like bombing machines. In the past few days they have excelled
at this, and the results are there for the entire world to see. Gaza
is licking its wounds, just like Lebanon before it, and almost no
one pauses for a moment to ask whether all this is necessary, or
unavoidable, or whether it contributes to Israel's security and
moral image. Is it really the case that our pilots return safely
to base, or are they in fact returning as callous, cruel and blind
people?

2009

23

And There Lie the Bodies

January 5, 2009

The legend, lest it be a true story, tells of how the late mathematician Professor Haim Hanani asked his students at the Technion to draw up a plan for constructing a pipe to transport blood from Haifa to Eilat. The obedient students did as they were told. Using logarithmic rulers, they sketched the design for a sophisticated pipeline. They meticulously planned its route, taking into account the landscape's topography, the possibility of corrosion, the pipe's diameter and the flow calibration. When they presented their final product, the professor rendered his judgment: "Everyone failed. None of you asked why we need such a pipe, whose blood will fill it and why the blood is flowing in the first place."

Regardless of whether this story is true, Israel is now failing its own "blood pipeline" test. Though Israel has been preoccupied with Gaza throughout the entire week, nobody has asked whose blood is being spilled and why. Everything is permitted, legitimate and just. The moral voice of restraint, if it ever existed, has been left behind. Even if Israel wiped Gaza off the face of the earth, killing tens of thousands in the process—as a Chechen laborer working in Sderot proposed to me—one can assume that there would be no protest.

They liquidated Nizar Ghayan? Nobody counts the twenty women and children who lost their lives in the same attack. There was a massacre of dozens of officers during their graduation

permitted, legitimate, just

ceremony from the police academy? Acceptable. Five little sisters? Allowed. Palestinians are dying in hospitals that lack medical equipment? Small potatoes. Whatever happened to the not-so-good old days of Salah Shehadeh? When we liquidated him in July 2002, we also killed fifteen women and children. At least back then, moral qualms were raised for a moment.

Here lie their bodies, row upon row, some of them tiny. Our hearts have turned hard and our eyes have become dull. All of Israel has worn military fatigues, uniforms that are opaque and stained with blood and which enable us to carry out any crime. Even our leading intellectuals fail to speak out about the havoc we have wreaked. Amos Oz urges: "Cease-fire now." David Grossman writes: "Hold your fire. Stop." Meir Shalev wants "a punitive operation." And not one word about our moral image, which has been horribly distorted.

The suffering in the south renders everything kosher, as if the horrible suffering in Gaza pales in comparison. Everyone is hungry for revenge, and that hunger is excused by the need for "deterrence," after it was already proven that the killing and the destruction in Lebanon did not achieve it.

Yes, I know, war is war. After all, they brought this on themselves. They are a terrorist organization and we are not. They want to destroy us and we seek peace. Still, is there nothing here that will stop this blood pipeline? Even those whose hearts are hardened by "moral righteousness" will have to momentarily halt the bombing machine and ask: Which Israel do we have before us? What will become of its standing in the world, the world which is now watching the events in Gaza? What are we inflicting on the moderate Arab regimes? And what of the simmering popular hatred we are sowing throughout the world? What good will emerge from all this killing and destruction?

It is doubtful that Hamas will be cut down to size as a result of this wretched war. Yet the face of the state has been cut down to size, as have civilian elites who are apathetic and scared. The "peace camp," if it ever existed, has been cut down to size. Attorney General Menachem Mazuz authorized the Ghayan killing, regardless of the cost. Haim Oron, the leader of the "new left-wing movement," supported the launch of this foolish war.

Nobody is coming to the rescue—of Gaza, or even of the remnants of humanity and Israeli democracy. The statesmen, the jurists, the poets, the authors, academia, and the news media—all pitch black over the abyss. When the time comes for reckoning, we will need to remember the damage this war did to Israel: The blood pipeline it laid has been completed.

24

A Different Patriotism

January 8, 2009

One could go to the sources and quote Leo Tolstoy, for example: "Patriotism in its simplest, clearest, and most indubitable signification is nothing else but a means of obtaining for the rulers their ambitions and covetous desires, and for the ruled the abdication of human dignity, reason, and conscience, and a slavish enthrallment to those in power. And as such it is recommended wherever it is preached. Patriotism is slavery."

And also: "How can we speak of the reasonableness of men who promise in advance to accomplish everything, including murder, that the government—that is, certain men who have attained a certain position—may command?" One can also resort to talk about "the last refuge of a scoundrel." But there is another way: to admit that you, too, are a patriot.

One could also quote an e-mail from Mahmut Mahmutoglu, in Turkey: "You are one of the most beautiful voices . . . I have yet to see or hear from Israel. . . . Tonight, after reading your article, I have come to have hope for peace and believe that humanity will prevail." And there is also Robert, the talk-backer from Israel, who responded to that same article of mine by writing, "I am not a doctor, but that man is sick." Or the reader George Radnay, one of hundreds, who wrote from New York: "Internal exile, à la Russie, should be instituted in Israel. You and other enemies of the human race should be exiled to Sderot. With no possibility to leave! Preaching hatred from

" Patriotism is slavery "

comfort and fat wallet, and with a passport; must be countered in the name of decency and peace."

The vast majority want to impose a total ban on all criticism, on every expression of alternative thinking, on every heretical sentiment, especially when it relates to this war, which I am already tired of calling accursed.

In this war, as in every war, an evil spirit has descended on the land. A supposedly enlightened columnist describes the terrible black smoke billowing out of Gaza as a "spectacular picture"; the deputy defense minister says that the many funerals in Gaza are proof of Israel's "achievements"; a banner headline, "Wounds in Gaza," refers only to the wounded Israeli soldiers and shamefully ignores the thousands of wounded Palestinians, whose wounds cannot be treated in the overflowing Gaza hospitals; the brainwashed commentators revel in the imaginary success of the incursion; the brainwashed soldiers are gung-ho for battle, for killing and for the mass destruction of the others, and maybe also, heaven forbid, of their own, and wipe out whole families, including the women and children; appalling Darfur-like images from Shifa Hospital show children dying on the floor; and the "patriotic" response is to shout: Three cheers! Hurrah! Well done! All hail the country that does these things!

Cry, the beloved country; that is not my patriotism, which is nevertheless supreme patriotism. In fact, the furious responses to every scrap of criticism give rise to the suspicion that perhaps some Israelis know deep within their desensitized hearts that something terrible is burning beneath their feet, that a vast conflagration is threatening to burst through the thick, stupefying, contorting and obfuscating fog that covers them. Maybe we are not as right as everyone promises us morning and night, maybe something horrific *is* happening in front of our wide-shut eyes. If Israelis were so sure of the rightness of their cause, why the violent intolerance they display toward everyone who tries to make a different case?

This is the time to ask the hard questions

This is precisely the time for criticism; there is no time more appropriate. This is exactly the time for the big questions, the fateful questions, the decisive questions. We should not just ask whether or not this or that move in the war is right, not just wonder whether we are progressing "according to plan." We also need to ask what is good about these plans. To ask whether Israel's very launching of the war is good for the Jews, good for Israel, and whether the other side deserves it. Yes, to ask about the other side is permissible even during war, perhaps above all during war. To know that the "children of the south" are not only the children who live in Sderot, but also the children of Beit Hanun, whose fate is immeasurably more bitter. To cringe with shame and guilt at the sight of Shifa Hospital is not treason; it is basic humanity. To take an interest in their fate, to ask whether their suffering is unavoidable, wise, just, moral and legitimate is an absolute necessity. To ask if things could have been done differently. To ask whether it would not have been more fitting to try a language other than the language of violence and unrestrained force that we invoke as a matter of routine, the only language in which we excel and in which we are articulate, believing that there is no other. This is the time to ask about our moral visage. This is exactly the time; there is no more appropriate time to cast doubt on the wisdom and the usefulness of this awful war, to look also at the blood and the suffering on the other side of the border, on the other side of humanity.

This cannot be solely the time for militarism, for the uniform and for the fanfare of war; this is also the time for humanity, for a critical view, for compassion. This is the time for a critical, humane, thinking media, not only a media that is insensitive, bestial and blind. This is the time for a media that reports the whole truth, not only our one-sided propaganda. This is precisely the time to inform the public about the whole picture, on both sides of the border, however harsh it may be,

Let the public know what's being done further in their name

without blurring it, without hiding anything, without sweeping the horror under the rug. Let the media consumers do as they wish with the information—delight in it, grieve over it—but let them know what is being done in their name. That is the role of everyone with eyes in his head, a brain in his skull and above all a beating heart in his chest.

People who make use of all their senses in trying times are no less patriotic than those whose restraint is lost, whose senses are dimmed and whose brains are washed. This is also the time for the patriot to say: Enough.

Patriotism? Who can measure what contributes more to the state, to which we are all bound by thick cords of steel, blood and feelings? Does joining the unseeing and stupefying chorus contribute or destroy; or could it be that the real contribution to democracy and the image of the state lies in raising the tough questions, precisely at this time? Is this the time to silence people and shatter the already fragile democracy here, or is it time for an attempt to preserve not only the right to be silent but also the right to shout out? Are the handful of people who are trying to preserve Israel's human image less concerned about the country's fate than the majority, who now see everything through the barrel of a gun?

And since when is a majority a guarantee of justice? Do we lack examples from history—modern and ancient, world history and Israel's history—in which the majority was fatally wrong and the minority ultimately right? Does a different voice, quiet and ostracized as it may be, but which nevertheless emerges from a darkened Israel to cast a ray of light into the world's bleakness, harm Israel's standing in the international community, or does it perhaps enhance it? A whistle in the dark is still a whistle, even in a time when the darkness into which we have plunged Gaza is nothing compared to the thick black darkness that has descended on Israel. Now is the time to ask the questions that will certainly be asked later, to voice the criticism that will undoubtedly be voiced afterward, but of course grossly late. And who is a traitor? Who will decide for us whether launching this war of folly is patriotism and rejecting it is treason? Will it be the militants, the nationalists, the chauvinists and the militarists among us? They, and only they? Do they have an exclusive franchise on patriotism? Or will it perhaps be the right-wing American Jews—those who become orgiastic whenever Israel kills and destroys—who decide? Is it not the case that the terrible damage that Israel is suffering because of this war is the greatest treason of all?

I have covered other wars. In the winter of 1993 I saw in besieged Sarajevo sights that have never been seen here—at least not until this war. How can I forget the old Bosnian woman who was digging in the earth with her fingers to find a few roots to eat? How can I forget our panicky running in the streets to escape the snipers, the bomb that struck the market and the music that blared, from an old radio on a heavily clouded evening in the midst of the darkness and the siege, "La ultima noche"? Last summer I covered the war in Georgia, where I saw refugees fleeing for their lives, carrying all their meager belongings in their hands, their eyes filled with fear and rage.

In both of those wars I felt remote, cut off, desensitized, a war correspondent who moves from one battle to the next. There we were not accomplices; my son's friends and my friends' sons were not accomplices to a crime. So it was easy for me, relatively and emotionally, to cover those wars. But not here and now. Here and now it is *my* war, *our* war, the war of us all, for which we all bear responsibility, of which we are all guilty. And therefore it is incumbent on us to make our voice heard, a different voice, a "hallucinatory" voice to the ears of the desensitized, a voice that is "traitorous," "base," "Jew-hating," "contemptible"—and different. This is not only our right, it is our supreme duty toward the state to which we are so bound, we patriotic scoundrels.

25

The Time of the Righteous

January 9, 2009

This war, perhaps more than its predecessors, is exposing the true deep veins of Israeli society. Racism and hatred are rearing their heads, as is the impulse for revenge and the thirst for blood. The "inclination of the commander" in the Israel Defense Forces is now "to kill as many as possible," as the military correspondents on television describe it. And even if that reference is to Hamas fighters, this inclination is still chilling.

The unbridled aggression and brutality are justified as "exercising caution." The frightening balance of blood—about 100 Palestinian dead for every Israeli killed—isn't raising any questions, as if we've decided that their blood is worth 100 times less than ours, in acknowledgement of our inherent racism.

Rightists, nationalists, chauvinists and militarists are the only legitimate *bon ton* in town. Don't bother us about humaneness and compassion. Only at the edges of the camp can a voice of protest be heard—illegitimate, ostracized and ignored by media coverage—from a small but brave group of Jews and Arabs.

Alongside all this rings another voice, perhaps the worst one of all. This is the voice of the righteous and the hypocritical. My colleague, Ari Shavit, seems to be their eloquent spokesman. This week, Shavit wrote in this paper,

> The Israeli offensive in Gaza is justified . . . Only an immediate and generous humanitarian initiative will prove that even during

the brutal warfare that has been forced on us, we remember that
there are human beings on the other side
("Israel must double, triple, quadruple its medical aid to Gaza,"
Haaretz, January 7).

To Shavit, who defended the justness of this war and insisted
that it mustn't be lost, the price is immaterial, as is the fact that
there are no victories in such unjust wars. And he dares, in the
same breath, to preach "humaneness."

Does Shavit wish for us to kill and kill, and afterward to set
up field hospitals and send medicine to care for the wounded?
He knows that a war against a helpless population—perhaps the
most helpless one in the world, one that has nowhere to escape
to—can only be cruel and despicable. But these people always
want to come out of it looking good. We'll drop bombs on residential buildings, and then we'll treat the wounded at Ichilov;
we'll shell meager places of refuge in United Nations schools,
and then we'll rehabilitate the disabled at Beit Levinstein. We'll
shoot and then we'll cry, we'll kill and then we'll lament, we'll
cut down women and children like automatic killing machines,
and we'll also preserve our dignity.

The problem is—it just doesn't work that way. This is
outrageous hypocrisy and self-righteousness. Those who make
inflammatory calls for more and more violence without regard
for the consequences are at least being more honest about it.

You can't have it both ways. The only "purity" in this war
is the "purification from terrorists," which really means the
sowing of horrendous tragedies. What's happening in Gaza is
not a natural disaster, an earthquake or flood, for which it would
be our duty and right to extend a helping hand to those affected,
to send rescue squads, as we so love to do. Of all the rotten
luck, all the disasters now occurring in Gaza are manmade—by
us. Aid cannot be offered with bloodstained hands. Compassion
cannot sprout from brutality.

Yet there are some who *still* want it both ways. To kill and destroy indiscriminately and also to come out looking good, with a clean conscience. To go ahead with war crimes without any sense of the heavy guilt that should accompany them. It takes some nerve. Anyone who justifies this war also justifies all its crimes. Anyone who preaches for this war and believes in the justness of the mass killing it is inflicting has no right whatsoever to speak about morality and humaneness. It is not possible to simultaneously kill and nurture. This attitude is a faithful representation of the basic, twofold Israeli sentiment that has been with us forever: to commit any wrong, but to feel pure in our own eyes. To kill, demolish, starve, imprison and humiliate—and to still be right, not to mention righteous. The righteous warmongers will not be able to allow themselves these luxuries.

Anyone who justifies this war also justifies all of its crimes. Anyone who sees it as a defensive war must bear the moral responsibility for its consequences. Anyone who now encourages the politicians and the army to continue will also have to bear the mark of Cain that will be branded on his forehead after the war. All those who support the war also support the horror.

26

My Hero of the Gaza War

January 11, 2009

My war hero likes to eat at Acre's famed Uri Burri restaurant. He thinks it's the best fish restaurant in the world, and he told me as much yesterday from the porch of the central Gaza City office building from which he has broadcast every day for the past two weeks, noon and night, almost without rest.

My war hero is Ayman Mohyeldin, the young correspondent for Al Jazeera English and the only foreign correspondent broadcasting during these awful days in a Gaza Strip that is closed off to the media. Al Jazeera English is not what you might think. It offers balanced, professional reporting from correspondents both in Sderot and Gaza. And Mohyeldin is the cherry on top of this journalistic sundae. I wouldn't have needed him or his broadcasts if not for the Israeli stations' blackout of the fighting. Since discovering this wunderkind from America (his mother is from the West Bank city of Tulkarm and his father from Egypt), I have stopped frantically changing TV stations.

Whoever recoils from the grotesque coverage by Channel 2's Roni Daniel is invited to tune in to this wise and considered broadcaster. Whoever recoils from our heroic tales, bias, whitewashed words, Rorschach images of bombing, IDF spokesman-distributed photographs, propagandists' excuses, self-satisfied generals and half-truths is invited to tune in. Whoever wants to know what is *really* happening, not only about a postponed wedding in Sderot and a cat forgotten in Ashkelon, is invited to tune in. Watching is sometimes hard, bloodcurdlingly hard, but reality is no less hard right now.

I have followed Mohyeldin throughout the war. Sporting a helmet and protective vest, and sometimes a Lacoste jacket, he stands on the roof, broadcasting in the most restrained tones, never getting excited or using flowery adjectives to describe what we're inflicting on Gaza, even when planes fly over him and bomb a house in the distance. Sometimes he crouches during a blast, his eyes perpetually glazed from fatigue, his face sometimes betraying helplessness.

At twenty-nine, he has already seen one war, in Iraq, but he says this war is more intense. He is frustrated that his broadcasts are carried virtually everywhere in the world except the United States, his own country, the place he thinks it is most important that these images from Gaza be seen.

"At the end of the day, if there is one country that can have influence, it's the United States. It's frustrating to know you're not reaching the viewers you would like to," he told me this week from the roof. On Friday he finally came down, for safety's sake, after the Israel Defense Forces bombed a neighboring media center. Is he afraid? "I'd be lying if I said I don't feel fear," he says. "But my obligation is greater than the fear."

Nor does he have a single bad word to say about Israel. He says he would gladly return to visit—after all, he's got friends here. We even set a dinner date at his favorite restaurant, for 6 p.m., after the war.

27

When the Guns Fall Silent

January 12, 2009

When the cannons eventually fall silent, the time for questions and investigations will be upon us. The mushroom clouds of smoke and dust will dissipate in the pitch-black sky; the fervor, desensitization and en masse jump on the bandwagon will be forever forgotten, and perhaps we will view a clear picture of Gaza, in all its grimness. Then we will see the scope of the killing and destruction, the crammed cemeteries and overflowing hospitals, the thousands of wounded and physically disabled, the destroyed houses that remain after this war.

The questions that will beg to be asked, as cautiously as possible, are who is guilty and who is responsible. The world's exaggerated willingness to forgive Israel is liable to crack this time. The pilots and gunners, the tank crewmen and infantry soldiers, the generals and the thousands who embarked on this war with their fair share of zeal will learn the extent of the evil and indiscriminate nature of their military strikes. Perhaps they will not pay any price. They went to battle, but others sent them.

The public, moral and judicial test will be applied to the three Israeli statesmen who sent the Israel Defense Forces to war against a helpless population, one that did not even have a place to take refuge, in what may be the only war in history against a strip of land enclosed by a fence. Ehud Olmert, Ehud Barak and Tzipi Livni will stand at the forefront of the guilty. Two of them are candidates for prime minister, the third is a candidate for criminal indictment.

It is inconceivable that they not be held to account for the bloodshed. Olmert is the only Israeli prime minister who sent his army to two wars of choice, all during one of the briefest terms in office. The man who made a number of courageous statements about peace late in his tenure has orchestrated no fewer than two wars. Despite all his talk of peace, this "moderate" and "enlightened" prime minister has been revealed as one of our greatest fomenters of war. That is how history will remember him. The "cash envelopes" crimes and "Rishon Tours" transgressions will make him look as pure as snow by comparison.

Barak, the leader of the party of the Left, will bear the responsibility for the misdeeds perpetrated by the IDF under his tutelage. His account will be burdened by the bombing and shelling of population centers, the hundreds of dead and wounded women and children, the frequent targeting of medical crews, the firing of phosphorus shells at civilian areas, the shelling of a UN-run school that served as a shelter for residents, who bled to death over days as the IDF prevented their evacuation by shooting and shelling. Even our siege of Gaza for a year and a half, whose ramifications are coming frighteningly into focus in this war, will be attributed to him. Blow after blow, all of these count in the world of war crimes.

Livni, the foreign minister and leader of the centrist party, will be remembered as the one who pushed for, legitimized and sat silent through all these events. The woman who promised "a different kind of politics" was a full partner in these crimes. This must not be forgotten.

In contrast to the claims being made otherwise, we are permitted to believe that these three leaders did not embark on war for electoral considerations. Any time is good for war in Israel. We set out for the previous war three months after the elections, not two months before. Will Israel judge these leaders harshly in light of the images emanating from Gaza? Highly doubtful. Barak and Livni are actually rising in the polls. The test awaiting these individuals will not be a local test. It is true that some international statesmen cynically applauded the blows Israel dealt. It is true that America kept silent, Europe stuttered and Egypt supported. But other voices will rise out of the crackle of combat.

The first echoes can already be heard. This past weekend, the UN and the Human Rights Commission in Geneva have demanded an investigation into war crimes allegedly perpetrated by Israel. In a world in which Bosnian leaders and their counterparts from Rwanda have already been put on trial, a similar demand is likely to arise for the fomenters of this war. Israeli basketball players will not be the only ones who have to shamefully take cover in sports arenas, and senior officers who conducted this war will not be the only ones forced to hide in El Al planes lest they be arrested. This time our most senior statesmen, the members of the war kitchen cabinet, are liable to pay a personal and national price.

I don't write these words with joy, but with sorrow and deep shame. Despite all the slack the world has cut us for as long as we can remember, despite the leniency shown toward Israel, the world might say otherwise this time. If we continue like this, maybe one day a new, special court will be established in the Hague.

28

Child's Play

January 15, 2009

The fighting in Gaza is "war deluxe." Compared with previous wars, it is child's play—pilots bombing unimpeded as if on practice runs, tank and artillery soldiers shelling houses and civilians from their armored vehicles, combat engineering troops destroying entire streets in their ominous protected vehicles without facing serious opposition. A large, broad army is fighting against a helpless population and a weak, ragged organization that has fled the conflict zones and is barely putting up a fight. All this must be said openly, before we begin exulting in our heroism and victory.

This war is also child's play because of its victims. About a third of those killed in Gaza have been children—311, according to the Palestinian Health Ministry; 270 according to the B'Tselem human rights group—out of the 1,000 total killed as of January 14. Around 1,550 of the 4,500 wounded have also been children, according to figures from the UN, which says the number of children killed has tripled since the ground operation began.

This is too large a proportion by any humanitarian or ethical standard.

It is enough to look at the pictures coming from Shifa Hospital to see how many burned, bleeding and dying children now lie there. History has seen innumerable brutal wars take countless lives. But the horrifying proportion of this war, a third of the dead being children, has not been seen in recent memory.

God does not show mercy to the children at Gaza's nursery schools, and neither does the Israel Defense Forces. That's how it goes when war is waged in such a densely packed area with a population so blessed with children. About half of Gaza's residents are under fifteen.

No pilot or soldier goes to war to kill children. Not one intends to kill children, but it also seems that in this war, neither did they intend *not* to kill children. Israel's pilots and soldiers went to war after the IDF had already killed 952 Palestinian children and adolescents since May 2000.

The public's shocking indifference to these figures is incomprehensible. A thousand propagandists and apologists cannot excuse this criminal killing. One can blame Hamas for the death of children, but no reasonable person in the world will buy this ludicrous, flawed propaganda in light of the pictures and statistics coming from Gaza.

One can say that Hamas hides among the civilian population, as if the Defense Ministry in Tel Aviv is not located in the heart of a civilian population, as if there are places in Gaza that are not in the heart of a civilian population. One can also claim that Hamas uses children as human shields, as if in the past our own organizations fighting to establish a country did not recruit children.

A significant majority of the children killed in Gaza did not die because they were used as human shields or because they worked for Hamas. They were killed because the IDF bombed, shelled or fired at them, their families or their apartment buildings. That is why the blood of Gaza's children is on our hands, not on Hamas's hands—and we will never be able to escape that responsibility.

The children of Gaza who survive this war will remember it. It is enough to watch Nazareth-born Juliano Mer Khamis's wonderful movie *Arna's Children* to understand what thrives amid the blood and ruin we are leaving behind. The film shows the children of Jenin—who have seen less horror than those of Gaza—growing up to be fighters and suicide bombers.

A child who has seen his house destroyed, his brother killed and his father humiliated will not easily forgive.

The last time I was allowed to visit Gaza, in November 2006, I went to the Indira Gandhi nursery school in Beit Lahia. The schoolchildren drew what they had seen the previous day: an IDF missile striking their school bus, killing their teacher, Najweh Halif, in front of their eyes. They were in shock. It is possible that some of them have now been killed or wounded themselves.

creating a whole new generation of terrorists

29

Thirsting for Blood
and Vengeance

January 16, 2009

Someone has to stop this rampant madness. Right now. It may seem as though the cabinet hasn't decided on the "third stage" of the war yet, Amos Gilad is discussing a cease-fire in Cairo, the end of the fighting seems close—but all this is misleading.

The streets of Gaza on Thursday looked like killing fields in the midst of the "third stage" and worse. Israel is arrogantly ignoring the Security Council's resolution calling for a cease-fire and is shelling the UN compound in Gaza, as if to show its real feeling toward that institution. Emergency supplies intended for Gaza residents are going up in flames in the burning warehouses. Thick black smoke, rising from the burning flour sacks and the fuel reserves near them, is covering the streets.

In the streets, people are running back and forth in panic, holding children and suitcases in their hands, helpless as the shells fall around them. Nobody in the diplomatic corridors is in any hurry to help those unfortunates who have nowhere to run.

The handful of journalists trying to cover the events, despite the outrageous media closure Israel has imposed, are also in danger. On Thursday the Israel Defense Forces shelled the media building they were in, and now they are all crowded into one office, as fearful and horrified as the rest of the scorched city's residents.

The BBC's Arabic correspondent, furious and alarmed, swears hoarsely that nobody fired from the building or around it. Meanwhile, in our television studios, there is rejoicing.

Is this war a "corrective experience"? This is asked by Rafi Reshef, who seems diabolically delighted by the fighting. Infrastructure Minister Benjamin Ben Eliezer tells him that the IDF and Israel Air Force have made great achievements. Nobody of course asks what is so great about these achievements, other than the killing, destruction and thousands of casualties in Gaza and the rockets that continue falling on Be'er Sheva—undermining every "achievement."

In the lobby of a luxury hotel, against the background of the horror show from Gaza, Foreign Minister Tzipi Livni explains, with intolerable arrogance, that the fire will stop "whenever Israel decides," on the basis of "daily situation evaluations."

UN Secretary General Ban Ki-moon, standing beside her, breaks protocol and denounces Israel with uncharacteristic vigor for its attack on the UN compound.

This is how Israel now looks to the outside world—its tanks in the burning streets of Gaza, more and more people being killed for nothing, tens of thousands of new refugees, an appallingly haughty foreign minister, and a growing clamor of condemnation and disgust from all over the globe.

Whether or not we have accomplished anything in the war, now only the thirst for blood and the lust for revenge speak out, together with the desperate longing for the "victory shot" on the backs of hundreds and thousands of miserable civilians— a picture that will never be achieved, even with another 100 assassinations of Hamas leaders, as on Thursday.

All those who supported this war and all those who objected to it should unite in the cry: Enough!

30

War By Any Other Name

January 16, 2009

Words, it is true, do not kill; but words can ease the work of killing. From the dawn of the Israeli occupation in the territories—by now an ancient dawn—or perhaps from the very establishment of the state, or maybe even from the revival of Hebrew, the language has been mobilized in active reserve service. There has been a permanent emergency call-up, and Hebrew has never doffed its uniform. In war after war, using doublespeak after doublespeak, words are on the front line. They don't shed blood, but they make the sight of it easier to take, sometimes even pleasurably so. They justify, validate, purify, polish and clean; often they also whip up, incite, inflame, push, urge and encourage—all in standard usage. Dry cleaning express, removing every stain instantaneously—our word-laundering is guaranteed.

We were hurled into this war armed with lines written by our national poet for the Hanukkah holiday, the holiday of the onset of this war: "Cast Lead," from a poem by Bialik. From now on, when kindergarten children sing, "My father lit me candles, and acted as my torch," people will remember this war, which some commentators are already calling "the most just in Israel's history," no less. But as for "war," the authoritative Even-Shoshan dictionary defines it as "an armed clash between armies, a conflict between state bodies (nations, states) in battle operations with the use of weapons and by force of arms." The

Litani Operation (Lebanon, March 1978), a large-scale action that lasted three full months, never gained the national honor of being considered a war. Even the "Second Lebanon War" was not given that official name until half a year after it ended. This time we were quicker and more determined. The forces had not yet raided at dawn, the planes had not yet finished bombing the graduation ceremony of the traffic police—leaving behind dozens of bleeding young bodies—and we were already calling it a war. For the time being, it is a nameless war; yes, afterward the ministerial committee for ceremonies and symbols will convene to give it an appropriate name. The First Gaza War, perhaps? Surely it will not be the last.

True, the dictionary raises doubts. This is certainly not "an armed clash between armies." After all, which army is fighting us, exactly? The army of Qassams and tunnels? It's even hard to call it "a conflict between nations and states in battle operations," because the battles are not actually battles, and one of the sides is not exactly a state—is barely half a nation, it has to be admitted. Still, war. What difference does it make if a senior officer in a reserve unit was quoted this week in *Haaretz* as saying, "It was a superb call-up and training exercise"? For us it's a war. For months we longed for it; oh, how we longed for the "big operation" in Gaza. No one talked about "war" then, but look, a war was born. *Mazel tov.*

There was nothing left to chance about this war. We went to "war" because that single, highly charged word serves infinite goals, all of them as just and as justified as the war itself. Say "war," and you say heroism and sacrifice. Add some grit, mobilization and of course the inevitable bereavement, and it's ready: war's verbal arsenal.

"Heroism and bereavement" was the headline the militant freebie *Israel Today* used in one of its combat editions. In war, as in "war," there is also "victory." Let the IDF win this war! But win over whom? How to win? Just win. But the goals of the

War change more quickly than a chameleon changes color—one day it's to stop the firing of the Qassams, and when that doesn't work, we switch goals. Now we have moved to a war against smuggling and tunnels. Maybe also a war of pressure on Egypt. And of course a war against Hamas, most of which is aimed at and strikes—just our bad luck—the helpless civilian population whose only connection to Hamas, if at all, was in the voting booth.

In war it is also necessary to upgrade the enemy's strength. First we are fed information for months on end about the Hamas arms buildup and its military sophistication, including bunkers and missiles from Tehran and Damascus, and now Ahmed Jabari is being called the "Hamas chief of staff." Lieutenant General Jabari, chief of the General Staff of the army of the semi-hollow Qassams. And why did we bomb the Islamic University in Gaza City? Because that is where the Palestinians' version of the Rafael Arms Development Authority was based, the Israeli press reported. That's where they develop drones that carry ammunition and bunker-busting missiles, not only lathes for machine-tooling. We built up their strength, and so heightened our victory and sweetened its taste.

In real wars, silence is permitted: Keep silent yourself and silence others. It's not just permitted, it's obligatory. Here is another good reason to call this a war. War makes it possible to mobilize, to call to the flag and unite the ranks of the people, who most of the time are more interested in the seacoast of Antalya than in any West Bank outpost. Only in war are we permitted to have media that sound more like the briefing room of the IDF spokesman. In war, propaganda is all right. Using the word "war" also validates war crimes, which might be prohibited in just a plain operation. If it's war, then let's go all the way: white phosphorus shells in the streets and artillery against population shelters, hundreds of women and children killed, strikes against rescue units and supply services. Hey, this is war, right?

War also gives rise to poetry about its heroism. True, we will never again have songs like the ones we had after the Six-Day War. Arik Lavie will no longer sing the lyrics of Yoram Taharlev: "We are past Rafiah, like you wanted, Tal, against the enemy we charged, and those who fell, fell. We passed by the fallen, we ran forward, Tal." (Major General Israel Tal commanded the division that captured Gaza in 1967.) It's true that we will never again sing "Nasser is waiting for Rabin, ay, ay, ay," or "Sharm al-Sheikh, we have come back to you again." But songs there will be, for sure. We have already had one rhymester wit in this war: "Hamas in Damascus is disconnected, the leadership in Gaza is dejected, the military wing is defecting, Hamas is screaming as expected." Cute, eh? (Lyrics as recited by the cabinet secretary, Oved Yehezkel, in a press briefing on Sunday about the briefing to the cabinet by the director of Military Intelligence.) Whoever the wag is, we already have our first war song, as boastful as "Nasser is waiting for Rabin."

The swaggering lyrics go hand in hand with doublespeak. "The houses have to be distanced from the border," a learned military analyst explained incisively last week, referring to what needs to be done in Rafah along the "Philadelphi" route. "To distance the houses from the border," as though these were homes marked for conservation in the old Sarona neighborhood of Tel Aviv, on which the Kirya—the defense establishment compound—now stands. Why, you just slide them onto tracks and move them a few meters down the road. Has the learned analyst seen the Rafah homes opposite Philadelphi in recent years? Most of them have long since been reduced to rubble. People lived in them, a great many people, who now have nowhere, but nowhere, to go. Now there are hundreds more ruined homes that we have "distanced from the border," so to speak.

We "liberated" the territories, "preempted" the terrorists and "preserved order," the order of the occupation; we consolidated

the occupation with a "civil administration," being careful not
to cause a "humanitarian disaster," jailed people in "administra-
tive detention," killed with "neighbor procedure," murdered
with "rules of engagement" and liquidated "senior figures in
Hamas"; children "died from their wounds," adults were killed
with "rubber bullets," a six-year-old child who is killed is a
"youth," a twelve-year-old who is killed is a "young man" and
both are "terrorists"; we established a "crossings unit," which is
a network of roadblocks, and a "coordination and liaison direc-
torate," which hardly coordinates or liaises between anything;
we killed "gunmen" and "wanted individuals" and people
"required for questioning," all of them "ticking bombs."

Now we have a "humanitarian corridor" and an equally
"humanitarian" cease-fire. People "in shock" exist only in
Israel; no one has gone into shock in Gaza. "Children of the
south" live only in Sderot. Hamas fighters are "terrorists," and
"Hamas activists," too, are not entitled to the honorific title of
"noncombatants," so their fate is the same. Every postman of
the Palestinian postal service, every policeman, every government accountant and maybe also every doctor working in
Hamas's non-civil administration is considered an activist of the
organization and therefore is to be killed before he kills us.

Our air force bombs and levels "targets," sometimes also
"structures"; never houses. Israel demands a "security zone" in
Gaza, and security is always ours, only ours. Only my colleague
at *Haaretz*, Amira Hass, dares, with characteristic courage, to call
the tens of thousands of newly homeless people in Gaza—made
homeless by us—"refugees" for the second and third time in
their lives; only Hass dares to call them "displaced persons," a
term that is so heavily charged and fraught with history. But
these DPs have nowhere to go to escape the horrors of the
"war."

31

An Open Response to A. B. Yehoshua

January 18, 2009

Dear Bulli,

Thank you for your frank letter and kind words. You wrote it from a "position of respect," and I, too, deeply respect your wonderful literary works. But, unfortunately, I have a lot less respect for your current political position. It is as if the mighty, including you, have all succumbed to a great and terrible conflagration that has consumed any remnant of a moral backbone.

You, too, esteemed author, have fallen prey to the wretched wave that has inundated, stupefied, blinded and brainwashed us. You're actually justifying the most brutal war Israel has ever fought, and in so doing you are complicit in the fraud that "the occupation of Gaza is over," as well as justifying mass killings by evoking the alibi that Hamas "deliberately mingles between its fighters and the civilian population." You are judging a help-less people denied a government and army—which includes a fundamentalist movement using improper means to fight for a just cause, namely the end of the occupation—in the same way you judge a regional power, which considers itself humanitarian and democratic, but which has shown itself to be a brutal and cruel conqueror. As an Israeli, I cannot admonish their leaders while our hands are covered in blood, nor do I want to judge Israel and the Palestinians in the same way you have.

The residents of Gaza have never had ownership of "their own piece of land," as you have claimed. We left Gaza because of our own interests and needs, and then we imprisoned them. We cut the territory off from the rest of the world and the occupied West Bank, and did not permit them to construct an air or sea port. We control their population registrar and their currency—and having their own military is out of the question—and then you argue that the occupation is over? We have crushed their livelihood, besieged them for two years, and you claim they "have expelled the Israeli occupation"? The occupation of Gaza has simply taken on a new form: a fence instead of settlements. The jailers stand guard on the outside instead of the inside.

And no, I do not know "very well," as you wrote, that we don't mean to kill children. When one employs tanks, artillery and planes in such a densely populated place, one cannot avoid killing children. I understand that Israeli propaganda has cleared your conscience, but it has not cleared mine, or that of most of the world. Outcomes, not intentions, are what count— and those have been horrendous. "If you were truly concerned about the death of our children and theirs," you wrote, "you would understand the present war." Even in the worst of your literary passages—and there have been few of those—you could not conjure up a more crooked moral argument: that the criminal killing of children is done out of concern for their fates. "There he goes again, writing about children," you must have told yourself this weekend, when you read my most recent article. Yes, it must be written. It must be shouted out. It is done for both our sakes.

This war, in your opinion, is "the only way to induce Hamas to understand." Even if we ignore the condescending tone of your remark, I would have expected more from you. I would have expected a renowned writer to be familiar with the history of national uprisings: They cannot be put down forcibly.

Despite all the destructive force we used in this war, I still can't see how the Palestinians have been influenced; Qassams are still being launched into Israel. They and the world have clearly taken away something else from the last few weeks—that Israel is a dangerous and violent country that lacks scruples. Do you wish to live in a country with such a reputation? A country that proudly announces it has gone "crazy," as some Israeli ministers have said in regard to the army's operation in Gaza? I don't.

You wrote that you have always been worried for me because I travel to "such hostile places." These places are less hostile than you think, especially if one goes there armed with nothing but the will to listen. I did not go there to "tell the story of the afflictions of the other side," but to report on our own doings. This has always been the very Israeli basis for my work.

Finally, you ask me to preserve my "moral validity." It isn't *my* image I wish to protect, but that of the country which is equally dear to us both.

In friendship, despite everything,

Gideon Levy

32

We've Won Nothing, Lost Everything

January 22, 2009

On the morrow of the return of the last Israeli soldier from Gaza, we can determine with certainty that they all went out there in vain. This war ended in utter failure for Israel.

This goes beyond the profound moral failure—which is a grave matter in itself—but pertains to its inability to reach its stated goals. In other words, the grief is not complemented by failure. We have gained nothing in this war save hundreds of graves (some of them very small), thousands of maimed people, much destruction and the besmirching of Israel's image.

What seemed like a predestined loss to only a handful of people at the onset of the war will gradually emerge as such to many others, once the victorious trumpeting subsides. The initial objective of the war was to put an end to the firing of Qassam rockets. This did not cease until the war's last day; it was only achieved *after* a cease-fire had already been arranged. And defense officials estimate that Hamas still has 1,000 rockets.

The war's second objective, the prevention of smuggling, was not met either. The head of the Shin Bet security service has estimated that smuggling will be renewed within two months.

Most of the smuggling that is going on is meant to provide food for a population under siege, and not to obtain weapons. But even if we accept the scare campaign concerning the smuggling, this war has served to prove that only poor quality, rudimentary weapons passed through the smuggling tunnels connecting the Gaza Strip to Egypt.

Israel's ability to achieve its third objective—deterrence—is also dubious. Deterrence, my foot. The deterrence we supposedly achieved in the Second Lebanon War has not had the slightest effect on Hamas, and the one supposedly achieved now isn't working any better: The sporadic firing of rockets from the Gaza Strip has continued over the past few days.

The fourth objective, which remained undeclared, was not met either. The IDF has not restored its capability. It couldn't have, not in a quasi-war against a miserable and poorly equipped organization relying on makeshift weapons, whose combatants barely put up a fight.

The heroic descriptions and victory poems written abut the "military triumph" will not serve to change reality. The pilots were flying on training missions and the ground forces were engaged in exercises that involved joining up and firing weapons. The describing of the operation as a "military achievement" by the various generals and analysts who offered their take on the operation is just plain ridiculous.

We have not weakened Hamas. The vast majority of its combatants were not harmed, and popular support for the organization has in fact increased. Their war has intensified the ethos of resistance and determined endurance. A country that has nursed an entire generation on the ethos of a few versus many should know to appreciate that by now. There was no doubt as to who was David and who was Goliath in this war.

The population in Gaza, which has sustained such a severe blow, will not become more moderate now. On the contrary, the national sentiment will turn even more than before against the party that inflicted the blow—the State of Israel. Just as public opinion leans to the right in Israel after each attack against

us, so it will in Gaza following the mega-attack that we carried
out against them.

If anyone was weakened because of this war, it was Fatah,
whose flight from Gaza and abandonment of it have now been
given special significance. The succession of failures in this war
needs to include, of course, the failure of the siege policy. For a
while now, we have known that this is ineffective. The world
boycotted, Israel besieged and Hamas ruled (and is still ruling).

But this war's balance, as far as Israel is concerned, does not
end with the absence of any achievement. It has placed a heavy
toll on us, which will continue to burden us for some time.
When it comes to assessing Israel's international situation, we
must not allow ourselves to be fooled by the support parade
of Europe's leaders who came in for a photo-op with Prime
Minister Ehud Olmert.

Israel's actions have dealt a serious blow to public support for
the state. While this does not always translate into an immediate
diplomatic situation, the shockwaves will arrive one day. The
whole world saw the images and was shocked, even if most
Israelis were left cold.

The conclusion is that Israel is a violent and dangerous country, devoid of all restraints, blatantly ignoring the resolutions
of the United Nations Security Council and not giving a hoot
about international law. The investigations are on their way.
Graver still is the damage this will visit upon our moral spine.
It will come from difficult questions about what the IDF did in
Gaza, which will occur despite the blurring effect of recruited
media.

So what was achieved, after all? As a war waged to satisfy the
considerations of internal politics, the operation has succeeded
beyond all expectations. Likud Chair Benjamin Netanyahu is
getting stronger in the polls. And why? Because we could not
get enough of the war.

33

No Moderates Left

January 25, 2009

The three leading candidates for prime minister are extremists.
Tzipi Livni and Ehud Barak went to war in Gaza and are therefore as radical as can be. Benjamin Netanyahu is more radical in
rhetoric only.

We must not be led astray in this election campaign and
consider both Livni and Barak as moderates, in contrast to the
"extremist" Netanyahu. This is a deception. Kadima and Labor,
the center and left-wing parties, have led Israel into two awful
wars within two years. Netanyahu has yet to go to war once.
True, he speaks more radically than the other two, but so far it
has only been words, while the "moderates" have taken radical,
aggressive action.

"Bibi is unreliable and terribly right-wing," Kadima's electoral broadcast asserts. Is he? Livni and Barak are just the same.

None of the people involved in the Gaza war can speak of
peace now. Those who delivered such a brutal blow to the
Palestinians, only to sow more hatred and fear among them,
have no intention of making peace. Those responsible for firing
white phosphorous shells into a civilian population and destroying thousands of homes cannot talk the following day about two
states living peacefully side by side.

In one fell swoop, Ehud Olmert, who issued some of the
bravest statements ever made in these parts about ending the
occupation, single-handedly turned them into a cynical babble

of hollow clichés. Who will now believe that he wanted peace? And who will believe Barak or Livni?

This war unmasked Livni, the woman who had promised us "different politics." She, who as foreign minister was supposed to show Israel's sunny side to the world, chose to present an arrogant, violent and brutal face. During the war she boasted that Israel was acting "savagely," threatened to let Hamas "have it" and announced that the cease-fire would come into effect "whenever Israel decides."

As far as she was concerned, there was no world, no United States and Europe, no UN Security Council, and no bleeding and defeated other side—only Israel would decide. No foreign minister has ever spoken like this before.

In her pathetic attempts to assume the masculine, militaristic, even macho posture of someone who would know what to say if the telephone rang at 3 a.m., Livni was exposed as a failed foreign minister, whose words and deeds are no different from those espoused by the radical militaristic men around her. No self-respecting voter who considers himself an upstanding centrist could vote for her. Whoever votes for Kadima will be voting for the right, which is eager to embark on any war and risk the accompanying crimes.

Voting for Labor also means voting for the war and its horrors. This war's marshal, Ehud Barak, has forever deprived himself of the moral right to talk of coexistence, political arrangements and diplomacy. If he really believed in those ideas, he would have given them a chance before going to war, not afterward. Barak took the army to war and Barak must pay for it, together with his "left-wing" party, which joined the most radical, far-right parties in supporting the move to outlaw Israel's Arab parties.

Avigdor Lieberman, Netanyahu, Livni and Barak are one—they all voted in support of an undemocratic decision. And don't be alarmed by Lieberman—he, too, only talks. But at least he does so honestly, while Barak fires off salvos and deceives.

Granted, these impostors still enjoy the support of world leaders, but for many people around the globe, they have become warmongers and suspected war criminals. Their diplomatic immunity will protect them—but who wants those leaders, with their bloodied hands, to represent us?

No less severe is the fact that there are no ideological differences between the candidates. Let Barak and Livni step up and explain what the hell sets them apart. What ideological argument are they conducting, apart from bickering about who should be credited for the war?

Facing them is Netanyahu—what does he have to offer? "Economic peace"? After this war, which wasn't enough as far as he is concerned, his doctrine sounds even more ludicrous than ever.

This is how we're going into the elections—with three leading parties that are hardly different from each other.

We always used to say, "There aren't any moderates in the Arab world." Now we are the ones who don't have any. Vote as you will, but don't fool yourself: Every ballot cast for Kadima, Labor or Likud is an endorsement of the last war and a vote for the next one.

34

The Silence of the Jurists

February 1, 2009

One silence, of all the shameful silences, has thus far roared especially loud—the silence of the jurists. Forty-one thousand attorneys in the State of Israel are entrusted with protecting its image as a lawful state, and this large and grand army has once again strayed from its function. There is a deep suspicion throughout the world that Israel carried out a series of war crimes, and the jurists of our country are holding their peace.

Where, for instance, is Aharon Barak when we really need him? Where are his colleagues, the former justices of the Supreme Court, who knew very well how to raise their voices when Justice Minister Daniel Friedmann threatened to harm the apple of their eye, and who now hide in their cowardly silence?

Where is Mishael Cheshin, who threatened to cut off the hand of anyone who raised it against the Supreme Court, no less; who now, with a heavy shadow being cast before us, does not say a word?

Do they not know that disproportionately harming a civilian population, supply convoys and medical crews, the use of white phosphorus in the midst of population centers and indiscriminate bombings are considered war crimes? What is their response to their enraged colleagues around the world? Are they convinced that Israel carried out these crimes or not? In either case, their voices are vital and their silence is abominable.

This war nearly did not make it onto the agendas of a majority of jurists in Israel. One look at the (Hebrew) Web site of the Israel Bar Association shows that the latest issues with which it is preoccupied are "The reservist soldier and his rights," "Discounts and benefits for business owners in the south," "Payment of membership fees—now by way of the bar" and "Flower design, a fun-filled workshop for lawyers in the southern district."

Not one word about the issue of war crimes. The Israel Bar cannot be bothered with it. With the exception of a few courageous lawyers, nobody is disturbed by the worrying legal aspects of the war. The killing of hundreds of children is not a sufficient reason to cry out when one is busy with flower design.

There is only one group now preoccupied with the war: the members of the Israel Defense Forces international law division, who continue to serve their bosses with piercing obedience, legitimizing every criminal act. They have already stated, for instance, that the criminal bombardment of a police academy graduation ceremony is acceptable in the eyes of international law. They have also ruled that picking up the telephone and calling those whose houses are about to be destroyed is sufficient to warrant this cruel form of collective punishment, which is also a war crime.

Now their commander, Colonel Pnina Sharvit-Baruch, is about to join the staff of lecturers at Tel Aviv University's Law Faculty, where she will present her doctrine of "devious jurisprudence that permits mass killing," in the words of the jurist Professor Haim Ganz, to students who will be happy to hear that Israel's filthy hands are as clean as a baby's.

This is not a case of one lawyer-colonel's opinion—as the faculty heads demagogically claim—but her deeds. It is feared that she is an accomplice to the commission of war crimes, and as such ought to be disqualified from teaching. Her addition to the faculty will serve as encouragement to those advocating an academic boycott against Israel. Her prospective students will continue to be educated according to the inglorious tradition of silence and legitimization: The jurists of Israel are always ready to keep quiet or legitimize any military operation. The judicial establishment has been enlisted—or, to be more precise, has itself enlisted—and it has a hand in the act.

Whoever honestly followed the events of the war knows that the question is no longer whether crimes were committed, but who bears the responsibility for them. Legal minds the world over are now diligently preparing legal cases detailing crimes allegedly committed, and only here do the reactions range from silence to legal propaganda.

How do the most important jurists around the world see what our lawyers have hidden from view? Is there no unequivocal, universal law on the matter? Does Israel have its own standard? Can everything be legitimized? Can international law be twisted and distorted, covered up with a Band-Aid to the point where mass killing and destruction are given a stamp of justification by our leading-light towers of justice? One could expect that of the brainwashed officers and soldiers, the media and public opinion—all of those who believe everything is permitted. But where, for goodness sake, are the defenders of the law?

We are left with a defense minister and a chief military rabbi who will hand down verdicts. Ehud Barak is calling for the liquidation of terrorists while they are in the bathroom; the chief military rabbinate is calling on soldiers to behave with cruelty. And the jurists? Don't disturb them during their moment of rest. They are busy processing membership payments for the Israel Bar.

35

Waltz with Bashir Is Propaganda

February 21, 2009

Everyone now has his fingers crossed for Ari Folman and all the creative artists behind *Waltz with Bashir* to win the Oscar on Sunday. A first Israeli Oscar! Why not?

However, it must also be noted that the film is infuriating, disturbing, outrageous and deceptive. It deserves an Oscar for the illustrations and animation—but a badge of shame for its message. It was not by accident that when Folman won the Golden Globe, he didn't even mention the war in Gaza, which was raging as he accepted the prestigious award. The images coming out of Gaza that day looked remarkably like those in Folman's film. But he was silent. So before we sing Folman's praises, which will of course be praise for us all, we would do well to remember that this is not an antiwar film, nor even a critical work about Israel as militarist and occupier. It is an act of fraud and deceit, intended to allow us to pat ourselves on the back, to tell ourselves and the world how lovely we are.

Hollywood will be enraptured, Europe will cheer and the Israeli Foreign Ministry will send the movie and its makers around the world to show off the country's good side. But the truth is that this film is propaganda. Stylish, sophisticated, gifted and tasteful—but propaganda nonetheless. A new ambassador of culture will now join Amos Oz and A. B. Yehoshua, and he too will be considered fabulously enlightened—so different from the bloodthirsty soldiers at the checkpoints, the pilots who bomb residential neighborhoods, the artillerymen who shell women and children, and the combat engineers who rip up streets. Here, instead, is the opposite picture—animated, too—of enlightened, beautiful Israel, anguished and self-righteous, dancing a waltz, with and without Bashir. Why do we need propagandists, officers, commentators and spokespersons who will convey "information" when we have this waltz?

The waltz rests on two ideological foundations. One is the "we shot and we cried" syndrome: Oh, how we wept, yet our hands did not spill this blood. Add to this a pinch of Holocaust memories, without which there is no proper Israeli self-preoccupation. And a dash of victimization—another absolutely essential ingredient in public discourse here—and *voilà*! You have the deceptive portrait of 2008 Israel, in words and pictures.

Folman took part in the Lebanon war of 1982, and two dozen years later he remembered to make a movie about it. He is tormented. He goes back to his comrades-in-arms, gulps down shots of whiskey at a bar with one, smokes joints in Holland with another, wakes his therapist pal at first light and goes to see him for another session—all to free himself at long last from the nightmare that haunts him. And the nightmare is always ours, ours alone.

It is very convenient to make a film about the first, and now remote, Lebanon war: We already sent one of those, *Beaufort*, to the Oscar competition. And it's even more convenient to focus specifically on Sabra and Chatila, the Beirut refugee camps.

Even way back, after the huge protest against the massacre perpetrated in those camps, there was always the declaration that, despite everything—including the green light given to our lackey, the Phalange, to execute the slaughter, and the fact that it all took place in Israeli-occupied territory—the cruel and brutal hands that shed blood were not our hands. Let us lift our voices in protest against all the savage Bashir-types we have known! And yes, a little against ourselves, too, for shutting our eyes, perhaps even showing encouragement. But still: That blood, that's not us. It's them, not us.

We have not yet made a movie about the other blood, which we have spilled and continue to allow to flow, from Jenin to Rafah—certainly not a movie that will get to the Oscars. And not by chance.

In *Waltz with Bashir*, the soldiers of the world's most moral army sing out something like: "Lebanon, good morning. May you know no more grief. Let your dreams come true, your nightmares evaporate, your whole life be a blessing."

Nice, right? What other army has a song like this, and in the middle of a war? Afterward they go on to sing that Lebanon is the "love of my life, the short life." And then the tank, from inside of which this lofty and enlightened singing emanates, crushes a car, turning it into a smashed tin can, and then pounds a residential building, threatening to topple it. That's how we are: singing and wrecking. Where else would you find sensitive soldiers like these? It would really be preferable for them to shout with hoarse voices: "Death to the Arabs!"

I saw *Waltz* twice. The first time was in a movie theater, and I was bowled over by the artistry. What style, what talent! The illustrations are perfect, the voices are authentic, the music adds so much. Even Ron Ben Yishai's half-missing finger is accurate. No detail is omitted, no nuance blurred. All the heroes are heroes, superbly stylish, like Folman himself: articulate, trendy, up-to-date left-wingers—so sensitive and intelligent.

Then I watched it again, at home, a few weeks later. This time I listened to the dialogue and grasped the message that emerges from behind the talent. I became more outraged from one minute to the next. This is an extraordinarily infuriating film precisely *because* it is done with so much talent. Art has been recruited here for an operation of deceit. The war has been painted with soft, caressing colors—as in comic books, you know. Even the blood is amazingly aesthetic, and suffering is not really suffering when it is drawn in lines. The soundtrack plays in the background, behind the drinks and the joints and the bars. The war's fomenters were mobilized for active service of self-astonishment and self-torment.

Boaz is devastated at having shot twenty-six stray dogs, and he remembers each of them. Now he is looking for "a therapist, a shrink, shiatsu, something." Poor Boaz. And poor Folman, too: He is devilishly unable to remember what happened during the massacre. "Movies are also psychotherapy"—that's the bit of free advice he gets. Sabra and Chatila? "To tell you the truth? It's not in my system." All in such up-to-the-minute Hebrew you could cry. After the actual encounter with Boaz in 2006, twenty-four years later, the "flash" arrives, the great flash that engendered the great movie.

One fellow comes to the war on the Love Boat, another flees it by swimming away. One sprinkles patchouli on himself, another eats a Spam omelet. The filmmaker-hero of *Waltz* remembers that summer with great sadness: It was exactly then that Yaeli dumped him. Between one thing and the other, they killed and destroyed indiscriminately. The commander watches porn videos in a Beirut villa, and even Ben Yishai has a place in Ba'abda, where one evening he downs half a glass of whiskey and phones Arik Sharon at the ranch and tells him about the massacre. And no one asks who these looted and plundered apartments belong to, damn it, or where their owners are and what our forces are doing in them in the first place.

That is not part of the nightmare.

What's left is hallucination, a sea of fears, the hero confesses on the way to his therapist, who is quick to calm him and explain that the hero's interest in the massacre at the camps derives from a different massacre: at the camps from which his parents came. Bingo! How could we have missed it? It's not us at all, it's the Nazis, may their name and memory be obliterated. It's because of them that we are the way we are. "You have been cast in the role of the Nazi against your will," a different therapist tells our hero reassuringly, as though evoking Golda Meir's remark that we will never forgive the Arabs for making us what we are. What we are? The therapist says that we shone the lights, but "did not perpetrate the massacre." What a relief! Our clean hands are not part of the dirty work, no way.

And besides that, it wasn't us at all: How pleasant to see the cruelty of the Other. The amputated limbs that the Phalange— may their name be obliterated—stuff into the formaldehyde bottles, the executions they perpetrate, the symbols they slash into the bodies of their victims. Look at them and then look at us: We never do things like that. *exonerates ISR*

When Ben Yishai enters the Beirut camps, he recalls scenes of the Warsaw ghetto. Suddenly he sees through the rubble a small hand and a curly haired head, just like that of his daughter. "Stop the shooting, everybody go home!" the commander, Amos, calls out through a megaphone in English. The massacre comes to an abrupt end. Cut.

Then, suddenly, the illustrations give way to the real shots of the horror of the women keening amid the ruins and the bodies. For the first time in the movie, we not only see real footage, but also the real victims. Not the ones who need a shrink and a drink to get over their experience, but those who will remain bereaved for all time, homeless, limbless and crippled. No drink and no shrink can help them. And that is the first (and last) moment of truth and pain in *Waltz with Bashir*.

36

"They Told Me Daddy Died"

February 26, 2009

As the war in Gaza raged, Israel Defense Forces reservists apparently thought anything was permissible: It was possible, maybe even necessary, to kill innocents in the West Bank. Under cover of war, they thought, they could also kill a handcuffed Palestinian.

After all, they could always claim he tried to steal their weapons—never mind that he was bound with plastic handcuffs that were practically impossible to get out of. A bullet in the stomach from close range ended the life of Yasser Temeizi, thirty-five, who had a work permit and had held jobs in Israel for all of his adult life; in the past year he had worked for the Harash company in Ashdod. He was a young father who'd never gotten into any trouble with the IDF before. The soldiers arrested him for no reason, beat him for no reason in front of one of his small children and finally executed him for no reason.

A month and a half has passed since this horrifying incident, and the army's criminal investigations division is still looking into the case. An investigation that could have been completed in an hour is going on interminably. Not a single Palestinian was questioned, as usual; not a single soldier was arrested—and most likely none will be—also as usual. The reservist soldiers who killed Temeizi have likely already been sent back home; perhaps they returned feeling good about their experiences and about doing their national duty. Granted, they didn't take part in the war in Gaza, but they killed, too. Why not? Herewith, as a service to them, is the story of the consequences of their actions, which senior IDF officers have already termed "a grave incident" that involved "a series of serious failures."

Yasser Temeizi, a conscientious and hard-working laborer, lived in the village of Idna, west of Hebron. He was the husband of Haife and the father of seven-year-old Firas and two-year-old Hala. For fifteen years, he got up every morning and went to work in Israel. In recent months he worked in Ashdod, for the Harash company, which builds cargo compartments for trucks. On his last payslip, it says: "Type of worker: Autonomy"—in the language of the occupation. "Amount paid: NIS 3,935.73." Upon the outbreak of the military operation in Gaza, Temeizi's employers asked him not to come to work until things calmed down. But he still had to support his family, so he made his way to the "slave market" in Kiryat Gat, hoping to find odd jobs. This is what he was doing on the morning of January 13.

On that day, Ehud Barak was trying to promote a week-long "humanitarian cease-fire," the Paratroops advanced toward Gaza City and a seventh Palestinian medical worker was killed by Israeli fire. At 5:30 that morning, Temeizi set out for Kiryat Gat, his work permit in his pocket. He returned home about four hours later; he hadn't found any work. His mother Naife made him a light breakfast, and then Temeizi asked his seven-year-old son Firas if he'd like to come with him to the family olive grove about three kilometers west of their house, a few hundred meters east of the separation fence, in the territories. Father and son loaded water and food onto the family's donkey and began riding toward the grove. If there was no employment to be had in Israel, at least they could work on the olives, they thought.

They arrived at the grove and got to work. Suddenly, a military jeep appeared and four soldiers got out. Firas saw them approaching his father. There was a verbal exchange between the men, but it was in Hebrew and Firas didn't understand what it was about. A minute later, he saw the soldiers shoving his father down to the ground and handcuffing him from behind. The soldiers ordered Firas to go home. His father also told him to go; the frightened little boy started running the long distance back toward home. On the way he was attacked by dogs, he says, and some shepherds, his neighbors, saved him from them. That was the last time Firas saw his father alive. Handcuffed and on the ground, but alive.

Eyewitnesses told Temeizi's father Saker that they'd seen soldiers kicking his bound and blindfolded son. The witnesses tried to intervene, but the soldiers shooed them away, brandishing their rifles. Musa Abu Hashhash, a reputable field researcher for the B'Tselem human rights organization, heard similar testimonies. Eventually, according to the witnesses, the soldiers put Temeizi on a jeep and drove off. This was the last time the Palestinians saw him alive.

Firas meanwhile made it home and reported that his father had been arrested. The family wasn't that concerned at first: The false arrest of a Palestinian is a matter of routine. They were sure Yasser, who had all the required permits and had never been in any trouble, would be released promptly and return home. But the hours passed and still Temeizi didn't return. Around four in the afternoon, neighbors reported that he had been killed and that his body was at Al Ahli Hospital in Hebron. Abu Hashhash rushed to the hospital and saw the body; he says he noticed handcuff marks on the wrists. The entry wound was in the stomach and the exit wound was in the thigh, which, according to experts, means that Temeizi was shot while sitting. Point-blank. An autopsy was performed at the Abu Dis pathology institute, and Abu Hashhash received the results. He said the reported cause of death was extensive bleeding.

Temeizi was not dead when he arrived at the hospital, but he died shortly thereafter. It may have been possible to save him had he received medical care in time. Ten days after the incident, Yuval Azoulay wrote a report on the incident in *Haaretz*. It appears that shortly after the killing, an IDF investigation was held with the participation of division commander Brigadier General Noam Tibon and brigade commander Colonel Udi Ben-Moha, who raised the prospect that "a series of failures" occurred on the part of the reservists who killed Temeizi. It was established that he had been brought, handcuffed, to the Tarqumiya checkpoint, and from there he was taken to a nearby army base.

The soldiers killed him in a room, without eyewitnesses, after he tried—so they claim, of course—to steal their weapons. No one explained how a handcuffed man could steal a weapon, or why the response should be a point-blank shooting.

Military sources told Azoulay that "the manner in which the incident was handled, particularly in regard to summoning of assistance for the wounded man, indicates there were serious failures. This is a very serious incident and one can't help thinking that if a regular force was stationed there, it would not have happened. The reservist soldiers are simply not familiar with or trained for such scenarios and such situations."

What kind of training is needed for such situations? Do soldiers really need to be trained not to shoot a handcuffed prisoner? Do they truly need to be trained to immediately summon medical care for someone who is gravely wounded?

The IDF spokesman told us officially this week, a month and a half after the incident: "The matter is under investigation by the criminal investigations division. Once the investigation is complete, the findings will be relayed to the military prosecutor."

Firas enters the bereaved household in Idna, a blue UNICEF book bag on his back. In a soft, chirpy voice, he tells the story of his last day with his father. He recounts the donkey ride to the family's olive grove, the soldiers who knocked his father down before his eyes and how he made his way home alone, scared by the barking dogs.

"Later on they told me that Daddy died," the boy says quietly, the trauma evident on his face. Just so the soldiers who killed a handcuffed man, and their commanders and investigators, should know.

37

Nothing But Lies

March 19, 2009

The lie, like a loaded gun, appeared in the opening of the first act. At the July 2, 2006 cabinet meeting, a week after Gilad Shalit was abducted, Prime Minister Ehud Olmert said, "I want to say something about the soldier's release: We shall not negotiate with Hamas on releasing prisoners, directly or indirectly." A prime minister's word.

Olmert's first lie was enough to denounce his complete conduct in the Shalit affair, but we tend to forgive any lie, even one so blatant, if uttered by the prime minister.

This firm statement did not stop Olmert from saying, in the same breath, "We'll do everything to bring about Shalit's release—and when I say everything, I mean everything. Everything possible, everything necessary." Nobody pointed out the contradiction.

That, too, was a lie, as Uri Blau reported in *Haaretz* yesterday. Secret IDF documents show that finding Shalit was not a first priority. Since then, the lies have been fired off, volley after volley: brainwashing, distorting and deceiving, with the media's consent and sponsorship. Meanwhile, Shalit rotted in captivity.

Olmert's "we'll do everything" began with Operation Summer Rains, which was payback for the abduction. Twenty Palestinian parliament members and eight ministers were abducted from their homes and imprisoned as "bargaining chips," which didn't help matters one iota. In the course of the operation, we also killed 394 Gaza residents. If it doesn't do any good, at least it won't do any harm, we figured. It did not do any good, of course.

After that glorious operation, the negotiations that we would "never conduct" began, brokered by Palestinian Authority President Mahmoud Abbas and Egypt. On July 1, 2006, Hamas demanded the release of 1,000 prisoners. Since then, Hamas has not budged from its set price—no bargaining, haggling, reductions or end-of-season sale.

Israeli officials say that Hamas "toughened its stance." Hamas did not toughen its stance. If you ask the prime minister and security commentators why Hamas toughened its stance, they will explain that it was because of the tumultuous public campaign to free Shalit. The truth is that Hamas has not changed its position for 1,000 days. Before or after the Shalit family's protest tent. Blaming public opinion, then, is also a lie and a calumny.

The next big lie, after the talks with Hamas began, was that we were not negotiating with Hamas, but with Egypt. This was a redundant, despicable and harmful deception. Israel was negotiating with Hamas. Directly or indirectly, whether the organization recognizes our existence or not, Israel has been negotiating with Hamas for a long time. Let's refute this lie at least. After doing so, perhaps we will recognize that it's better to negotiate with Hamas directly, and not only about Shalit.

"We spared no effort, but we came up against a brutal, murderous, pitiless organization, devoid of basic human emotions, which was unwilling to meet the challenge," Olmert said on Tuesday, announcing defeat. A prime minister who launched an offensive on the besieged, helpless population in Gaza—during which 1,300 people were killed and 100,000 left homeless, by an army that acted with unrestrained violence—has no moral right to speak of brutality, murderousness and lack of pity.

Is Hamas devoid of human emotion? Maybe, but it is fighting for the release of its people, who have no chance of gaining their freedom in any other way but through a deal. Nothing could be more humane than that. Even the Israeli propaganda about the "price" of Shalit's release is based on a lie. Nobody can seriously argue that releasing 325 terrorists wouldn't harm Israel's security, but releasing 450 would. Would 125 men, closely watched by the Shin Bet, really make the difference?

Studies have shown that most of the prisoners released so far, especially those who spent many years in prison, did not return to terrorist activity. But the officials tell us a different story. And above all, who decided that releasing prisoners is an Israeli "surrender," while Shalit's continued imprisonment is a "victory"?

Now that lying has failed miserably, perhaps we should try something different. Let's tell the truth without any propaganda: Shalit's fate is important to us, but not important enough.

38

A New Consensus

March 12, 2009

Suddenly we're all in consensus: The recent war in Gaza was a failure. The *bon ton* now is to list its flaws. Flip-floppers say its "achievements" were squandered; leftists say the war "should never have started" and rightists will say the war "should have lasted longer." But on this they all agree: It was a blunder.

Because we consider the war to have been almost cost-free, with just thirteen Israeli dead, it will be the first in thirty-six years without a Commission of Inquiry formed in its wake.

Of course, the war's blunder was just as serious as its predecessors, but because we did more killing than being killed, because we caused more damage than we sustained, there's nothing deemed worthy of investigation.

It was all in vain: no progress made, no goal achieved, nothing. Deterrence was not reestablished, arms smuggling into Gaza was not stopped, Hamas was not weakened and abducted Israel Defense Forces soldier Gilad Shalit was not freed. On these facts we all agree.

Moreover, we paid a huge price: Hamas is stronger, the injured Palestinian people are even more hateful toward us, and Israel is viewed as a pariah in global public opinion, with rioting on a basketball court in Ankara where an Israeli team played and the banning of spectators from Israel's Davis Cup tennis encounter with Sweden in Malmö. We are the last of the rogue states.

Nobody has to answer for all this—neither the politicians who launched this crazy war nor the army commanders who were their contractors. No one will be impeached, never mind tried in court. Israel's aggressive and violent war machine won't even suffer a tiny dent.

And what of the cheerleaders who sat on the sidelines of this hellish nightmare? Perhaps we should at least hold them accountable. They sat in their television studios and at their newspaper desks. Oh, how the commentators were excited and stirred excitement! They goaded and urged, pushed and applied pressure, begging for more and more war. For months they had been clamoring for their "wide-scale operation," their hearts' desire. When their wish came true, they cheered in support and whistled in excitement.

Do not take their actions lightly. They could have had an immense influence over the feeble politicians and graying officers. "Strike out at them!" their baritone voices echoed from one part of the country to the other. They asserted that it was a just and successful war without peer. They covered the brilliant military maneuvers with gusto, iniquitously hid the horrors, presented an unrestrained offensive against a nonexistent enemy as a two-sided war, described troops' unchallenged advances as real combat and a military maneuver carried out on the back of a helpless population as a success.

They appeared in their studios with their mouths still flecked with foam left over from their previous successful horror show, the Second Lebanon War. The retired generals and Tarzan commentators, whose coverage of the war in Lebanon was an abominable failure, recycled the same clichés and propaganda dictates. No one considered replacing them after their previous failure. They learned nothing and forgot nothing, and the vast majority of us nodded thoughtlessly at their words, as though they came from above.

The déjà vu is striking: Again, just like after the Second Lebanon War, they suddenly became the war's biggest critics, only after it had already ended—a matter of timing.

Showing no remorse and much vanity, they now shamelessly admit that the war whose praises they sang has failed. Why did it fail? Because we didn't kill enough people, they explain. If we would have given it a little push and killed 200 more children or massacred 500 more women, *then* we would have achieved victory.

None of them are asked what would have happened had the war continued. Would Shalit have been freed? Would Hamas have waved the white flag? Would the Palestinian people have joined the Zionist movement?

Now, get ready for the next treat. They've already begun to clamor for a new war in Gaza or Lebanon, whichever comes first. When they get what they ask for, they will return to their studios. In the beginning they will offer their support for the war, and then they will come out against it.

No one will hold them accountable for their vile acts, and there will be nothing new under the sun.

39

The Most Moral Army
in the World

March 22, 2009

What shock, what consternation. *Haaretz* revealed grave accounts by officers and soldiers describing the killing of innocent Palestinian civilians during the war in Gaza. The Israel Defense Forces spokesman was quick to respond that the IDF had no prior or supporting information about the events in question, the defense minister was quick to respond that "the IDF is the most moral army in the world" and the military advocate general said the IDF would investigate.

All these propagandistic and ridiculous responses are meant not only to deceive the public, but also to offer shameless lies. The IDF knew very well what its soldiers were doing in Gaza. It has long ceased to be the most moral army in the world. Far from it—it will not seriously investigate anything.

The testimonies from the graduates of the Oranim premilitary course were a bolt from the blue—accounts of soldiers butchering a woman and two of her children, of shooting and killing an elderly Palestinian woman, how they felt when they murdered in cold blood, how they destroyed property and how there was not even fighting in this war that was not a war.

But this is neither a bolt nor blue skies. Everything has long been known by those who wanted to know, those who, for example, read Amira Hass's dispatches from Gaza in this paper. Everything started long before the assault on Gaza.

The soldiers' transgressions are an inevitable result of the orders given during this brutal operation, and they are the natural continuation of the last nine years, when soldiers killed nearly 5,000 Palestinians, at least half of them innocent civilians, nearly 1,000 of them children and teenagers.

Everything the soldiers described from Gaza—everything— occurred during these blood-soaked years as if they were routine events. It was the context, not the principle, that was different. An army whose armored corps has yet to encounter an enemy tank and whose pilots have not faced an enemy combat jet in thirty-six years has been trained to think that the only function of a tank is to crush civilian cars, that a pilot's job is to bomb residential neighborhoods.

To do this without any unnecessary moral qualms, we have trained our soldiers to think that the lives and property of Palestinians have no value whatsoever. It is part of a process of dehumanization that has endured for dozens of years—the fruits of the occupation.

"That's what is so nice, as it were, about Gaza: You see a person on a road . . . and you can just shoot him." This "nice" thing has been around for forty years. Another soldier talked about a thirst for blood. This thirst, too, has been with us for years. Ask the family of Yasser Temeizi, a thirty-five-year-old laborer from Idna who was killed by soldiers while bound, or Mahdi Abu Ayash, a sixteen-year-old boy from Beit Umar who was found in a vegetative state, another victim of recent days, far from the war in Gaza.

Most of the soldiers who took part in the assault on Gaza are youths with morals. Some of them will volunteer for any mission. They will escort an old woman across the street or rescue earthquake victims. But in Gaza, when faced with the "inhuman" Palestinians, the package will always be suspicious, the brainwashing will be stupefying and the core principles will change. That is the only way they can kill and engage in wanton destruction without deliberating or wrestling with their consciences, not even telling their friends or girlfriends what they did.

Regarding the statement of one soldier—"As much as we talk about the IDF being an army of values, let's just say this is not the situation on the ground, not on the battalion level"— the IDF has long ceased to be an army of "values," not on the ground, not in the battalion, not in the senior command. When an army does not investigate thousands of cases of killing over many years, the message to the soldiers is clear, and it comes from the top.

Our Teflon chief of staff, Gabi Ashkenazi, cannot wash his hands of this affair. They are bloody. What the soldiers of the preparatory academy described were war crimes, crimes for which they should be tried. This will not happen, save for the grotesque spectacle of "principled probes" in an army that killed 1,300 people in 25 days and left 100,000 homeless. Military police investigations will not lead to anything.

The IDF is incapable of investigating the crimes of its soldiers and commanders, and it is ridiculous to expect it to do so. These are not instances of "errant fire," but of deliberate fire resulting from a direct order. These are not "a few bad apples," but rather the spirit of the commander, and this spirit has been bad and corrupt for quite some time.

Change will not come without a major shift in mindset. Until we recognize the Palestinians as human beings, just as we are, nothing will change. If it did, the occupation would collapse, God forbid. In the meantime, prepare for the next war and the next round of horrific testimonies about the most moral army in the world.

40

Another Wonderful Summer

July 19, 2009

Really, who needs all this? The US president is spending a considerable amount of his precious time and goodwill trying to be persuasive about the need to end the Arab–Israeli conflict. The Europeans are ready to act, half the world is waiting, but let's admit the truth: Why all the commotion about us? The settlers might scream and block highway intersections. The Israel Defense Forces would become less important, and the news could actually become boring. The vineyard in the Golan Heights is liable to close, as might the boutique winery in the settlement of Ofra.

Life in Israel is just peachy, and who wants to think about peace, negotiations, withdrawals, the price we have to pay and all this unnecessary mess? Cafés are bustling and restaurants are packed. People are vacationing. The markets are surging. Television dumbs us down, highways are jammed, and the festivals are blaring. La Scala performed in the park and Madonna is to follow, and the beaches are full of foreign tourists and locals. The summer of 2009 is wonderful. Why should we change things?

The Israelis aren't paying any price for the injustice of occupation. Life in Israel is immeasurably better than in most countries. The global financial crisis has hit Israel less hard than other places. We have poor people, but not like in the developing world, and the rich and middle class here have not been seriously harmed.

The security situation is also in good shape. No terrorist attacks. No Arabs. And when terrorism subsides, as it has over the past several years, who remembers that there is a "Palestinian problem"? The army and Prime Minister Benjamin Netanyahu can continue to scare us with the terrorism threat, but for the moment, at least, it doesn't exist. The Iranian nuclear threat is also just a vague idea at the moment. Life in Israel is currently secure.

True, every few years a wave of violence erupts, but it usually happens in the country's outskirts and doesn't interest anyone in the center. Qassam rockets in Sderot or Katyushas in Kiryat Shmona? Who cares? These will be followed by another period of quiet, like now. The separation fence, the media, our education system and political propaganda do a great job of creating an illusion to make us forget what we need to forget and hide what needs to be hidden. The troubles are there and we are here, and here life is a bowl of cherries, if not a blast. Like Switzerland? No, even better.

[handwritten marginal note: create illusion security]

We always knew how to add a measure of significance to the pleasures of life. We practice the cult of security, society's true religion, and we perpetuate the memory of the Holocaust. You can enjoy yourself in Israel and also play the victim; party and gripe. Where else is there a place like this?

The Israelis don't pay any price for the injustice of the occupation, so the occupation will never end. It will not end a moment before the Israelis understand the connection between the occupation and the price they will be forced to pay. They will never shake it off on their own initiative, and why should they?

Even the cruelest terrorist attacks to befall the country haven't instilled an understanding among the Israelis about the connection between cause and effect, between occupation and terrorism. Thanks to the media and the politicians—two of the worst agents for dumbing down and blinding Israeli society—we learned that the Arabs were born to kill, the whole world is against us, anti-Semitism determines how Israel is dealt with and there is no connection between our actions and the price we pay.

Neither an international blockade nor terrible bloodletting appear to be on the horizon, to our great fortune. So why should we worry? It's true that the world is beginning to scowl at Israel. But so what? Israelis are convinced that the world hates us anyway. As long as we are not deprived of the world's pleasures, there is no reason to worry. Try to ask Israelis why they are ostracized and you will immediately hear scorn about the world, rather than any self-criticism, God forbid. The Israelis are not only enjoying themselves, they are also very satisfied with themselves—over their level of morality and that of their army and state.

All this really could have been peachy, if not for the fact that blindness is dangerous and the not-so-good ending is known in advance. Sure, it's another wonderful summer in Tel Aviv—and Gaza and Jenin—but some part of the world will blow up in our faces. And then we will pretend to be amazed, miserable victims, as we so like to be.

Chronology

September 12, 2005   End of the Israeli army's withdrawal from the Gaza Strip, after thirty-eight years of occupation, in line with Israeli Prime Minister Ariel Sharon's unilateral disengagement plan.

January 25, 2006   Hamas wins a majority of votes in the Palestinian legislative elections.

February 18, 2006   Investiture of the new Palestinian parliament.

February 19, 2006   The Israeli government adopts a series of measures collectively punishing the population of the occupied territories, among which is a freeze on the transfer of taxes and customs due to the Palestinian Authority.

March 29, 2006   Investiture of the Hamas government.

April 7, 2006   The European Union suspends direct financial aid to the Palestinian government, thereby bringing about the suspension of the salaries of more than 150,000 Palestinian civil servants. The Palestinian Authority is now on the verge of bankruptcy.

June 24, 2006   The Israeli army carries out a raid on the house of the Muamar family, in a village near Rafah and abducts two brothers, Osama, a doctor, and Mustafa, a student. The following day, a Palestinian commando unit attacks an Israeli frontier post, killing two soldiers and abducting another, Gilad Shalit.

June 28–November 26, 2006   The Israeli government launches a huge ground and air offensive in the Gaza Strip. Named Operation Summer Rains, the offensive encompasses a considerable number of military operations. Among them are Operation Locked Garden in Gaza City's Sajaya neighborhood, on August 26, and Operation Autumn Clouds, in the town of Beit Hanoun, from November 1–8.

July 12–August 14, 2006   The Second Lebanon War, or July War.

September 2, 2006   Widespread strikes by Palestinian civil servants demanding the payment of their salaries.

November 1–8, 2006   The Israeli ground and air offensive, Operation Autumn Clouds, concentrated on Beit Hanoun in the north of the Gaza Strip, kills 60 Palestinians, injuring 200.

November 26, 2006   After five months of Israeli military operations in the Gaza Strip, a Palestinian-Israeli ceasefire is concluded. Operation Summer Rains has killed almost 400 Palestinians and has destroyed much of Gaza's infrastructure, including the Strip's only electricity power plant.

September 19, 2007   Israel declares the Gaza Strip a "hostile entity," a decision taken after a vote by Israel's security council.

October 28, 2007   Israel imposes economic sanctions on the Gaza Strip.

November 26–28, 2007   At a US-brokered conference in Annapolis, Ehud Olmert and Mahmoud Abbas agree to conclude a peace treaty before the end of 2008.

February 27–March 3, 2008   Israeli army offensive against the Gaza Strip, dubbed Operation Hot Winter, is launched in response to the killing of an Israeli in a Palestinian rocket attack. More than 120 Palestinians are killed; 350 are wounded.

June 19, 2008   After months of Egyptian mediation, Israel and Gaza's Hamas government conclude a six-month ceasefire. Israel agrees to the gradual lifting of the blockades imposed on the Strip.

November 4, 2008   An Israeli infantry unit enters Gaza and shoots dead six Hamas gunmen. Hamas responds with rocket attacks into southern Israel.

December 19, 2008   With Israel failing to lift its blockade of the Gaza Strip, Hamas announces that it will no longer continue the ceasefire.

December 20, 2008   End of the six-month ceasefire between Israel and Hamas.

December 27, 2008   Israel launches a massive airborne offensive against the Gaza Strip. Operation Cast Lead is the biggest offensive of its kind in the Palestinian Territories since 1967. Its stated objective is to put an end to the firing of rockets into Israel. In the first days of the operation, at least 400 Palestinians are killed.

January 3, 2009   Following the airstrikes, Israel moves to the second stage of its operation. More than 9,000 soldiers start deploying in the north of the Strip accompanied by tanks and mobile artillery. Israeli army spokespeople indicate that this will be a prolonged ground offensive.

January 4, 2009   At a meeting of the UN Security Council, convened to discuss the Gaza situation, the member states are unable to reach agreement on the issue of the invasion.

January 6, 2009   Israeli bombardments hit three UN-managed schools: at least 43 Palestinians are killed and 100 wounded.

January 9, 2009   The UN Security Council votes to call for an immediate ceasefire.

January 17, 2009   Israel announces a unilateral ceasefire. The following day Hamas does the same, giving the Israeli army a week to withdraw from the Gaza Strip. According to Palestinian medical services, in three weeks the Israeli offensive has killed 1,330 Palestinians, of whom more than 430 are children, and left 5,450 wounded. On the Israeli side, 10 military personnel and 3 civilians have been killed, according to official figures.